EMPOWERED
TO LEAD

A Guide for Women Working in
Male-Dominated Industries

STACY WHITENIGHT

EMPOWERED TO LEAD

Contents

For The Jefas.

Author's Note

As a Latina who has been working in tech for over 20 years, my journey to leadership has been filled with both opportunity and challenge. I recognize that, at times, being white-presenting has afforded me access to spaces and experiences that many women like me are often denied. My father, who was not only white but wealthy, provided me with privileges that opened some doors, but learning to lead authentically has meant navigating the complexities of those privileges while staying true to my roots and values.

Leadership for me has been a process of unlearning what the world told me I should be, discovering who I truly am, and striking a balance between living a life shaped by capitalism and a desire to decolonize that very system. It's a delicate dance, and one I'm still learning.

Empowered to Lead reflects this personal journey of authenticity, growth, and self-discovery. My hope is that this book helps other women, especially those navigating male-dominated spaces, to break through barriers, lead authentically, and thrive in their careers without losing sight of who they are.

Thank you for being a part of this journey. I hope these pages inspire you to lead boldly and live fully, on your own terms.

Con corazón y valentía,
Stacy Whitenight

Introduction

This guide is crafted with a singular purpose: to empower women to not only survive but thrive in these environments. By providing practical strategies, actionable insights, and real-life stories from women who have walked the path before, this guide aims to equip you with the tools you need to confidently pursue your goals, assert your value, and achieve lasting success in any male-dominated field.

In the bustling hub of a leading tech company, Maria paused by the glass-walled conference room. Inside, a sea of suited figures leaned into the table's embrace - men exchanging brisk nods and firm handshakes. She noted the absence of a female presence, not with a sense of surprise, but as a stark reminder of her own daily odyssey. With each step she took through the sterile corridors, past her male counterparts' curious gazes, Maria carried the weight of silent expectation.

Instead of an office filled with grandiose speeches about breaking through barriers, she found solace in the small victories. A successfully coded program spoke volumes in the echo chamber of her male-dominated field. Her voice didn't carry the authoritative timbre of Sheryl Sandberg's, but in low, measured tones, she offered precise feedback to her team, found ways to streamline processes that hadn't been touched since their inception.

She met the challenges not with grand declarations but with the steady click-clack of her keyboard and the quiet persistence on her face - each wrinkle around her eyes a testament to a problem solved, an obstacle overcome.

On lunch breaks at a park bench under autumn's watchful eye, she exchanged knowing glances with another - Lydia from finance. Their shared smiles were not of defeat but recognition; each crumb from their sandwiches falling like breadcrumbs for those who would follow in their stead, mapping out paths less daunting.

One evening over coffee-stained blueprints and flickering fluorescent lights, they discussed not just problems but solutions. Their dialogue was devoid of fanfare yet brimming with determination. They sketched out mentorship programs, peer-to-peer networks -

an architecture for support that stretched beyond the company walls.

Maria's strides were not broadcasted across headlines; rather, they resonated in the quiet assurance of her colleagues - women who began to raise their hands more often in meetings or confidently negotiate their salaries. And when she listened closely on occasions where silence used to dwell, Maria could hear the faint symphony of progress - a chorus growing stronger by the day.

This guide is designed for women at every stage of their professional journey. Whether you're a recent graduate stepping into your first job, a mid-career professional aiming for a leadership role, or a seasoned expert seeking to leave a lasting impact, the strategies and insights offered here will support your ambitions. Regardless of your industry or role, if you're navigating a predominantly male workplace, this guide is for you. It's for those who seek not just to fit in but to stand out, to lead with confidence, and to inspire others along the way.

Overview of Challenges and Opportunities

Working in a male-dominated industry often comes with a unique set of challenges. From facing unconscious bias and stereotypes to overcoming feelings of isolation or so-called imposter syndrome, the road can be tough. Women in these environments may encounter obstacles such as limited access to mentorship, exclusion from key networks, or being overlooked for promotions and leadership roles. Within these challenges lie significant opportunities.

Women who succeed in male-dominated industries often emerge as trailblazers, leading the way for others to follow. The very act of overcoming these barriers can foster resilience, innovation, and leadership qualities that are invaluable in any professional setting. This guide will explore these challenges in depth, offering strategies to turn them into stepping stones for growth. It will also highlight the immense potential for women to drive change, influence company culture, and lead with authenticity and strength in spaces where they are underrepresented.

By embracing the opportunities within these challenges, women can not only advance their own careers but also contribute to a more inclusive and diverse workplace, paving the way for future generations. This guide is your companion on that journey, providing the knowledge and encouragement you need to succeed.

Chapter One

Understanding the Landscape

Male-dominated industries are sectors where men significantly outnumber women in the workforce, leadership roles, and decision-making positions. Fields such as technology, engineering, finance, construction, and manufacturing have historically been dominated by men due to a combination of social, cultural, and institutional factors. These industries often perpetuate a culture that favors traditional masculine traits, making it challenging for women to enter, thrive, and ascend to leadership roles.

The persistence of homogeneous dominance in these industries is rooted in longstanding stereotypes, gender roles, and structural barriers. Despite progress in gender equality, women continue to face obstacles such as unequal access to opportunities, lack of mentorship, and limited representation in leadership. These challenges are compounded by workplace cultures that may be less accommodating to women's needs and perspectives, leading to slower progress in achieving gender parity.

The Gender Gap

The gender gap in male-dominated industries is stark and far-reaching. Women, especially those from marginalized groups, face significant disparities in representation, pay, and leadership opportunities.

Representation

Women make up a small percentage of the workforce in many male-dominated fields. For example, women account for only about 25% of the tech workforce and 13% of engineers in the United States. The numbers are even lower for women of color. According to a 2022 report by the National Science Foundation, Latinas represent just 2% of workers in tech, while Black women make up 3% and Indigenous women accounts for less than 1%.

Pay Disparity

The gender pay gap remains a persistent issue, with women earning significantly less than their male counterparts. The American Association of University Women (AAUW) reports that, on average, women earn 82 cents for every dollar earned by men.

Again we see an even greater disparity for women of color—Black women earn 63 cents, Latinas 55 cents, and Indigenous women 60 cents for every dollar earned by white, non-Hispanic men. Asian women earn about 85 cents, though this average masks wide variations within different subgroups.

Leadership Roles

Women's representation in leadership roles is also limited. In 2023, only 28% of senior management roles globally were held by women, according to Grant Thornton's Women in Business report. For women of color, these numbers are even lower. In the Fortune 500 companies, there were only 41 women CEOs in 2023, with just a handful being women of color.

The Importance of Advocacy and Allyship

Given the disparities and challenges faced by women, particularly those from underrepresented groups, it is crucial to advocate for and become allies to others, even if you do not see yourself as a representative of these groups. Advocacy and allyship are essential in creating inclusive environments where all women can thrive. By supporting each other, we can help dismantle the barriers that perpetuate inequality.

Why Advocate?

Advocating for others helps to amplify voices that might otherwise be marginalized or overlooked. It ensures that diverse perspectives are considered in decision-making processes, leading to more equitable outcomes. Advocacy also helps to create a culture of inclusion, where differences are celebrated rather than seen as obstacles.

The Role of Allies

Allies play a critical role in challenging biases and stereotypes, supporting the professional development of underrepresented groups, and advocating for systemic change. Even if you do not belong to a specific group, your support can be a powerful force for change. Being an ally involves listening, learning, and taking action to address inequalities and support the success of others.

Cultural Dynamics and Bias

Cultural dynamics and bias within male-dominated industries can manifest in various ways, often making it difficult for women to feel valued and respected. These dynamics include unspoken rules, stereotypes, and biases that shape workplace culture and interactions.

- **Unspoken Rules**: In many male-dominated fields, there are unspoken expectations about how one should behave, communicate, and succeed. These rules often align with traditional masculine norms, such as assertiveness, competitiveness, and risk-taking. Women who do not conform to these norms may be unfairly judged or overlooked.

- **Stereotypes**: Stereotypes about women's capabilities and roles persist in many workplaces. Women may be seen as less competent in technical roles, less suited for leadership, or more emotional and less rational than their male counterparts. These stereotypes can lead to biased evaluations, exclusion from important projects, and limited opportunities for advancement.

- **Bias**: Both conscious and unconscious biases can affect how women are treated in the workplace. Unconscious bias, in particular, can lead to subtle yet pervasive forms of discrimination, such as being interrupted more frequently in meetings, receiving less credit for contributions, or being passed over for promotions. Addressing these biases requires awareness, education, and deliberate action to create a more equitable workplace.

The Importance of Self-Awareness

Self-awareness is a critical tool for personal and professional growth in navigating male-dominated industries. Knowing your strengths, values, and areas for growth allows you to navigate challenges with confidence and resilience.

Recognizing Your Strengths

Understanding what you bring to the table—whether it's technical expertise, leadership skills, or creative problem-solving—helps you to assert your value in the workplace. Celebrating your strengths can also combat feelings of imposter syndrome, reinforcing your belief in your competence.

Understanding Your Values

Your values guide your decisions and interactions. By aligning your actions with your core values, you can navigate the workplace with integrity and authenticity, even in the face of challenges. Knowing your values also helps you to identify environments and opportunities that resonate with your personal and professional goals.

Identifying Areas for Growth

Self-awareness also involves recognizing areas where you can improve. Whether it's developing new skills, enhancing your leadership capabilities, or learning to navigate office politics, being open to growth ensures that you continue to evolve and thrive in your career.

To thrive in any space, it is crucial to understand the unique challenges that come with them and utilize your strengths to your advantage. We owe a debt of gratitude to the women who have paved the way for us, as well as to our allies who share their valuable insights. Thanks to them, we now have access to the knowledge and techniques necessary to navigate these environments with confidence and determination.

Chapter Two

Build a Strong Foundation

Solidifying your own personal branding is more important than ever to distinguish yourself among an increasingly competitive market. Your personal brand is your reputation—it's how you present yourself to the world and how others perceive you in your industry.

In male-dominated fields, where women already face challenges in being seen and heard, a strong personal brand can be a powerful tool for standing out and asserting your value.

By investing in your personal brand, you take control of your professional narrative. You define how others perceive you and how you are positioned within your industry. With a strong personal brand, you can navigate male-dominated fields with confidence, resilience, and a clear sense of purpose.

In the echoing boardroom, Ana felt the weight of every gaze as she presented her quarterly report. Her voice never faltered, a practiced calm betraying none of the frustration that buzzed beneath her skin like static. Regardless of her composure, she caught Mark's smirk as he leaned back in his chair, arms crossed, a silent challenge.

Later in the break room, hushed whispers swirled around her like leaves in autumn wind. She poured herself a coffee, the black liquid a stark contrast to the sterile white mug. Choosing a seat apart from the clustering colleagues, she pulled out a small notebook filled with meticulously charted graphs and notes – her roadmap through an often unwelcoming terrain.

In the cubicle that she personalized with framed credentials and a single potted succulent, Ana's fingers paused above her keyboard. Screens flashed with lines of code – her domain where logic ruled over prejudice. She let out a measured breath and began typing, transforming complex problems into elegant solutions. Eyes on her screen but ears attuned to the office's pulse, she noted how conversations shifted when she walked by. Fortified by self-knowledge and an unshakeable sense of purpose,

Ana moved with deliberate steps. She understood the subtle game being played – one where credit was as currency and visibility was earned rather than given. A mentor once told her: "Your work speaks for you," and so she let it shout. Her projects were masterpieces of innovation and precision, yet they whispered secrets only those who listened closely could appreciate – lessons on determination etched into binary.

Ana always arrived earlier than most. The rising sun cast long shadows across her desk as she sketched out plans for personal branding akin to setting sail on open waters. On her monitor rested a digital collage of role models and visionaries – women whose success stories were lighthouses guiding her journey through stormy seas.

Months later, when asked about her career aspirations during a panel discussion, instead of reciting rehearsed platitudes, Ana shared her vision with actionable steps and clear objectives. Aspiring minds in the audience scribbled notes, their pens scratching like tiny drumbeats heralding change.

Through each action, each choice made with intention, Ana curated an image that resonated with strength and expertise. Her personal brand was not crafted from vanity but necessity. It was the armor she wore in a field where battles were fought on uneven ground and victories sweeter for their rarity.

Understanding Personal Branding

Personal branding is not just about creating a polished online profile or a catchy tagline; it's about consistently showcasing your unique qualities, values, and expertise. It's the sum of how you communicate your skills, experiences, and aspirations, both in person and online. A strong personal brand helps you to build credibility, establish authority in your field, and differentiate yourself from others.

Step 1: Crafting Your Personal Brand

- **Identify Your Unique Value Proposition**: Start by understanding what makes you unique. What skills, experiences, and qualities set you apart from others in your field? Your unique value proposition (UVP) is the core of your personal brand—it's the answer to the question, "Why should someone choose to work with you?" Reflect on your strengths, achievements, and the feedback you've received from colleagues and mentors. Use this to craft a clear, concise statement that defines what you offer and why it matters.

· **Define Your Core Values**: Your values are the guiding principles that influence your decisions and actions. They are an essential part of your personal brand because they reflect what you stand for and what others can expect from you. Take the time to identify your core values—whether it's integrity, innovation, collaboration, or another principle—and ensure that these values are evident in how you conduct yourself professionally.

· **Develop Your Personal Brand Statement**: Your personal brand statement is a succinct summary of who you are, what you do, and how you add value. It should be clear, compelling, and reflective of your UVP and core values. For example, a personal brand statement might be: "I am a strategic thinker with a passion for leveraging data to drive business growth. I help organizations unlock their potential by turning complex information into actionable insights."

Step 2: Communicating Your Personal Brand

· **Consistency Is Key**: Consistency is crucial in personal branding. Ensure that your personal brand is reflected consistently across all platforms and interactions, both online and offline. This includes your LinkedIn profile, social media presence, resume, portfolio, and even how you communicate in emails and meetings. A consistent personal brand helps to build trust and reinforces your professional identity.

· **Leverage Social Media**: Social media is a powerful tool for building and maintaining your personal brand. Platforms like LinkedIn, Twitter, and even Instagram can be used to share your expertise, network with industry peers, and engage in meaningful conversations. Regularly post content that aligns with your personal brand—whether it's thought leadership articles, industry news, or insights from your work. Engage with others by commenting on posts, sharing content, and joining relevant groups.

· **Network Authentically**: Networking is an essential part of building your personal brand, but it's important to approach it authentically. Focus on building genuine relationships rather than just collecting contacts. Attend industry events, participate in online forums, and connect with professionals who share your interests and values. When networking, be mindful of how you present yourself—ensure that your personal brand is reflected in how you introduce yourself, what you talk about, and how you follow up.

Step 3: Maintaining and Evolving Your Personal Brand

· **Stay Relevant**: The professional world is constantly evolving, and so should your personal brand. Stay current with industry trends, continue learning new skills, and adapt your personal brand as you grow in your career. Regularly review your personal brand statement and online profiles to ensure they accurately reflect your current skills, experiences, and goals.

· **Seek Feedback and Reflect**: Personal branding is not a one-time effort—it requires ongoing reflection and refinement. Seek feedback from colleagues, mentors, and peers to understand how your brand is perceived. Use this feedback to make adjustments and strengthen your brand. Reflect on your experiences, successes, and challenges, and consider how these can inform and enhance your personal brand.

· **Showcase Your Achievements**: Don't be shy about sharing your successes. Regularly update your online profiles, resume, and portfolio with your latest achievements, projects, and skills. Share case studies, testimonials, or examples of your work that demonstrate your expertise and the value you bring. Highlighting your achievements not only reinforces your personal brand but also positions you as a thought leader in your field.

The Impact of a Strong Personal Brand

A well-developed personal brand can have a significant impact on your career. It can open doors to new opportunities, enhance your credibility, and position you as a leader in your industry. In male-dominated fields, where women may need to work harder to be seen and heard, a strong personal brand is particularly valuable. It's your way of asserting your presence, showcasing your value, and standing out in a crowded and often challenging environment.

By investing in your personal brand, you take control of your professional narrative. You define how others perceive you and how you are positioned within your industry. With a strong personal brand, you can navigate male-dominated fields with confidence, resilience, and a clear sense of purpose.

Continuous Learning and Specialization

Technology is constantly advancing and industries are evolving at a rapid pace to keep up. In order to remain relevant and competitive in this environment, it is crucial to constantly seek out opportunities for learning and skill development. This is particularly important in male-dominated fields where innovation moves quickly and expectations are high. By actively pursuing knowledge and expertise, not only do you improve your own skills, but you also demonstrate your value as an asset in your industry.

The Need for Continuous Learning

Alex had always been passionate about their career in software engineering. When they first started, their skills were cutting-edge, and their knowledge of programming languages and software tools put them at the forefront of the industry. But as the years went by, Alex noticed something unsettling—the tools and techniques they once mastered were becoming obsolete. New technologies were emerging at a rapid pace, and the industry was shifting in ways they hadn't anticipated.

Determined not to be left behind, Alex realized they needed to make an intentional commitment to stay ahead of industry trends by regularly updating their skills. Alex began by enrolling in online courses to master the latest software and programming languages. They also attended industry conferences and webinars, absorbing information about emerging technologies and regulatory changes that were transforming the field.

This dedication to their own development paid off. When a leadership position opened up on a complex, cross-functional project, Alex was the first choice. Their up-to-date knowledge and ability to quickly adapt to new challenges made them the ideal candidate. They took on the role confidently, applying what they had learned to manage the project successfully.

But Alex didn't stop there. The more they learned, the more their problem-solving abilities expanded. Faced with a particularly challenging issue during the project, Alex was able to draw from a broad range of skills and ideas they had acquired through continuous learning. Their innovative approach not only solved the problem but also impressed the leadership team, who saw Alex as an indispensable part of the company's future.

Staying Ahead of Industry Trends

Industries such as technology, finance, engineering, and others are characterized by rapid advancements and shifting trends. Just like we see with Alex's experience above, what was once cutting-edge a few years ago might now be obsolete. Embracing a mindset and discipline of continuous learning allows you to stay ahead of these changes, ensuring that your skills and knowledge remain up-to-date. Whether it's mastering a new software, understanding the latest regulatory changes, or learning about emerging technologies, staying informed is key to maintaining your competitive edge.

Adapting to New Challenges

As your career progresses, you will encounter new challenges and opportunities that require different skills. Continuous learning equips you to adapt to these changes, whether it's taking on a leadership role, managing complex projects, or navigating cross-functional teams. By proactively learning new skills, you prepare yourself to meet these challenges head-on and excel in your career.

Enhancing Problem-Solving Abilities

The more you learn, the better equipped you are to solve complex problems. Continuous learning broadens your perspective, exposes you to new ideas, and enhances your ability to think critically. No matter what industry you find yourself in problem-solving is always highly valued, having a diverse skill set can make you an indispensable part of your team.

The Power of Specialization

Having a broad range of skills is valuable, but true career growth often comes from specializing in a specific area. Specialization allows you to carve out a niche, making you an expert in your field and setting you apart from the competition. This focused expertise not only enhances your credibility but also opens doors to unique opportunities and career paths that align with your interests and strengths. Here's why specialization can be a powerful tool for advancing your career:

Becoming an Expert

While continuous learning helps you stay adaptable, specialization allows you to carve out a niche in your field. By focusing on a specific area of expertise, you can develop a deep understanding of the subject matter, making you a go-to person for that particular skill or knowledge.

Specialization not only enhances your credibility but also increases your value in the job market. Employers and colleagues will see you as an expert, someone who can provide insights and solutions that others cannot.

Differentiating Yourself in a Competitive Market

Competition is fierce in the market and will continue to be moving forward. Specialization is a way to differentiate yourself from others. Whether it's becoming an expert in a particular technology, mastering a specific regulatory framework, or specializing in a niche area of your industry, having a unique skill set sets you apart from the competition. It also opens doors to opportunities that may not be available to those with more general knowledge.

Creating a Unique Career Path

When you have a unique skill or knowledge, this can also help you create a unique career path that aligns with your interests and strengths. By focusing on an area that you are passionate about, you can build a career that is not only successful but also fulfilling.

This differentiation allows you to take control of your professional journey, steering it in a direction that resonates with your goals and values.

Practical Steps for Skill Development and Specialization

Developing and specializing your skills is key to staying relevant and competitive in your industry. By focusing on the areas that matter most and continually expanding your knowledge, you can position yourself as a valuable asset in your field. Here are practical steps you can take to enhance your skills and deepen your specialization:

- **Identify Industry Needs**: Start by understanding the current and future needs of your industry. What skills are in demand? What problems need to be solved? What emerging technologies or trends are likely to shape the future of your field? By identifying these needs, you can focus your learning efforts on areas that will provide the most value.

· **Invest in Professional Development**: Take advantage of professional development opportunities such as workshops, conferences, online courses, and certifications. Many industries offer specialized training programs that can help you deepen your expertise in a particular area. Investing in your professional development is an investment in your future.

· **Leverage Online Learning Platforms**: The rise of online learning platforms has made it easier than ever to access high-quality educational resources. Websites like Coursera, Udemy, LinkedIn Learning, and others offer a wide range of courses that can help you develop new skills or specialize in a particular area. These platforms often provide flexible learning options, allowing you to learn at your own pace and fit education into your busy schedule.

· **Seek Mentorship and Guidance**: Mentorship is a powerful tool for skill development and specialization. Seek out mentors who have expertise in the areas you want to specialize in. They can provide guidance, share their experiences, and offer valuable insights that you might not find in a textbook or online course. Mentors can also help you navigate the challenges of your industry and provide support as you work to achieve your goals.

· **Apply What You Learn**: Knowledge is most valuable when it is applied. Look for opportunities to put your new skills into practice, whether it's through projects at work, volunteer opportunities, or side ventures. Applying what you learn reinforces your knowledge and helps you gain practical experience, making you more confident and competent in your specialized area.

The Impact of Skill Development on Your Career

Continuous learning and specialization have a profound impact on your career trajectory. They increase your adaptability, making you more resilient in the face of change. They enhance your credibility, positioning you as an expert in your field. And they open doors to new opportunities, allowing you to pursue a career path that is both successful and fulfilling.

In male-dominated industries, where the pressure to perform and compete is often intense, the ability to continuously learn and specialize is a significant advantage. It empowers you to stay relevant, navigate challenges with confidence, and differentiate yourself in a crowded market. By committing to skill development, you take control of your professional growth and set yourself up for long-term success.

Building a Robust Network of Mentors, Peers, and Allies

Alicia had always been a top performer in her engineering roles, but as she moved up the ranks in her male-dominated tech company, she started feeling isolated. She was often the only woman in the room during meetings, and while her ideas were solid, she noticed they didn't always gain the traction they deserved. Despite her accomplishments, Alicia felt like she was hitting an invisible ceiling, unable to break through to the leadership level she aspired to.

One day, after a particularly frustrating meeting where her proposal was brushed aside, Alicia decided she needed to approach her career differently. She had always focused on her technical skills and work ethic, but now she realized she needed something more—she needed a network.

Alicia started by attending industry events, which at first felt intimidating. She was surrounded by strangers, many of whom seemed to know each other already. But she pushed past the discomfort, reminding herself that everyone had to start somewhere. At one event, she struck up a conversation with another woman, Maria, who worked in a similar field but at a different company. They bonded over shared experiences and exchanged contact information. Maria mentioned a women's networking group she was a part of and invited Alicia to join.

Through Maria, Alicia was introduced to a mentor named Sarah, a senior executive who had navigated the tech industry for over two decades. Sarah was not only knowledgeable but also deeply supportive. She provided Alicia with invaluable advice on how to navigate office politics, how to assert her ideas more effectively, and even how to negotiate for better opportunities.

Alicia's peer network also began to grow. She connected with colleagues in her company and from other organizations who were at similar stages in their careers. They started meeting regularly, discussing challenges, sharing resources, and even collaborating on side projects that helped them all grow professionally. The camaraderie and mutual support from these peers gave Alicia a renewed sense of confidence.

But perhaps the most significant change came when Alicia began cultivating allies within her company. She identified a few male colleagues who were genuinely supportive of diversity and inclusion.

She engaged them in conversations about the challenges she faced and asked for their support in meetings. These allies began to amplify her voice in those critical rooms, backing up her ideas and ensuring they were given the attention they deserved.

With the support of her mentor, peers, and allies, Alicia's career began to take off in ways she hadn't anticipated. Her proposals were no longer overlooked, and she was given the opportunity to lead a high-profile project that showcased her skills. Eventually, she was promoted to a leadership position—one she had been eyeing for years.

Alicia's story is a testament to the power of networking. She learned that success in a male-dominated industry wasn't just about being the best at her job; it was also about building relationships with people who could support her, challenge her, and help her grow. By investing in her network, Alicia didn't just advance her career—she created a community that empowered her to thrive.

The Importance of Networking in Male-Dominated Industries

Networking is a critical component of career success, particularly in male-dominated industries where access to opportunities, information, and support can often depend on who you know. A robust network of mentors, peers, and allies can provide guidance, open doors, and offer the encouragement needed to thrive.

- **Access to Opportunities**: Networking provides access to opportunities that might not be advertised or readily available. In male-dominated fields, where women may be underrepresented, a strong network can help you tap into job openings, projects, or collaborations that might otherwise be out of reach. It's often through connections that new roles, speaking engagements, and leadership positions are discovered.

· **Support and Guidance**: Navigating a career in a male-dominated industry can be challenging, but having a network of supportive mentors, peers, and allies can make the journey easier. These connections can offer advice, share their experiences, and provide emotional support when you face setbacks or challenges. They can also serve as sounding boards for ideas, helping you to make informed decisions.

· **Visibility and Recognition**: Networking helps increase your visibility within your industry. By connecting with others, attending events, and participating in discussions, you raise your profile and become more recognizable to potential employers, collaborators, and leaders in your field. This visibility can lead to greater recognition of your work and contributions, which is particularly important in environments where women's achievements may be overlooked.

Building a Network of Mentors

Mentorship and coaching, while often used interchangeably, serve different purposes in your professional development. Coaching typically focuses on specific skills or goals, with a more structured, performance-driven approach. Mentorship, on the other hand, is a broader, more personal relationship that offers guidance, support, and wisdom drawn from the mentor's experiences.

Mentors help you navigate the complexities of your career, offering insights that extend beyond immediate tasks or goals. Building a strong network of mentors can significantly enhance your career journey, providing the long-term support and perspective needed to achieve your aspirations. Here's how to effectively identify, approach, and nurture mentorship relationships:

Identifying Potential Mentors

Mentors are individuals with more experience or expertise who can provide guidance and support as you navigate your career. To identify potential mentors, look for leaders in your industry whose careers you admire, who have overcome challenges similar to those you face, or who possess skills and knowledge you want to develop.

Mentors can be found within your organization, through professional associations, or even through online platforms like LinkedIn.

Approaching a Mentor

When approaching a potential mentor, be respectful of their time and clear about what you're seeking. Start by building a rapport, perhaps through an introductory email or a brief meeting, and express your interest in learning from their experiences.

Be specific about how their guidance could help you and suggest ways you could structure the mentorship relationship, whether through regular check-ins, advice sessions, or informal conversations.

Nurturing the Mentorship Relationship

A successful mentorship is a two-way relationship. While you will benefit from your mentor's insights, be sure to show appreciation for their time and expertise. Keep them informed about your progress, seek their advice on specific challenges, and be open to feedback.

Additionally, consider how you can contribute to the relationship, whether it's by offering your own insights, sharing resources, or helping them with a project.

Connecting with Peers

Peers are colleagues at a similar career stage who can offer mutual support, share experiences, and collaborate on projects. A strong peer network can provide camaraderie, help you navigate challenges, and offer fresh perspectives. In male-dominated industries, where women may be in the minority, a peer network can also create a sense of community and belonging.

Peer connections can be made in various settings, including within your workplace, at industry events, or through professional organizations. Online communities, such as LinkedIn groups, forums, or social media platforms, are also excellent places to connect with peers who share your interests and challenges. Additionally, consider joining or creating peer networking groups that focus on supporting women in your industry.

These relationships thrive on collaboration and mutual support. Look for opportunities to work together on projects, share resources, or exchange feedback. Celebrate each other's successes and offer encouragement during challenging times. By fostering a culture of collaboration rather than competition, you can build strong, lasting relationships that benefit all involved

Cultivating Allies

Allies are individuals who may not share your background or experiences but who support your efforts to succeed and advocate for diversity and inclusion. In male-dominated industries, allies can play a crucial role in challenging biases, opening doors, and creating a more inclusive workplace culture. They can amplify your voice, advocate for your ideas, and help to ensure that you have a seat at the table.

There are allies and disruptors at all levels of an organization and across different functions. They may be male colleagues who are committed to gender equality, leaders who champion diversity, or peers who understand the importance of inclusion. To engage allies, start by building relationships based on mutual respect and shared goals. Be open about the challenges you face and how they can support you in overcoming them.

Allies can be powerful partners in advocating for systemic change within an organization or industry. Collaborate with them to promote initiatives that advance diversity and inclusion, such as mentorship programs, diversity training, or policy changes. Encourage them to use their influence to challenge biases, promote fair practices, and support the advancement of underrepresented groups.

Maintaining and Expanding Your Network

Networking is an essential aspect of career development, but it's not a one-time effort. Unlike coaching, which often focuses on specific skills or goals within a set timeframe, networking is an ongoing process that requires consistent engagement and a long-term perspective. Building and maintaining strong connections can open doors to new opportunities, provide valuable support, and help you navigate your career more effectively.

Here's how to ensure your network remains vibrant and continues to grow over time:

Consistency and Engagement

- Networking is not a one-time activity; it requires ongoing effort to maintain and expand your connections. Regularly engage with your network by attending events, participating in discussions, and reaching out to your contacts.

- Stay in touch with mentors, peers, and allies, even when you're not seeking immediate support. This consistent engagement helps to keep relationships strong and ensures that you remain top of mind when opportunities arise.

Giving Back to Your Network

- Networking is a reciprocal process. As you benefit from the support of your network, look for ways to give back. Offer your time and expertise to others, provide introductions or referrals, and share resources that could be valuable to your connections. By contributing to your network, you build goodwill and strengthen your relationships.

Continuously Expanding Your Network

- As your career progresses, continue to expand your network by seeking out new connections and opportunities. Attend industry conferences, join professional organizations, and participate in online communities.

· When you are open to meeting new people and exploring different perspectives, you will unlock a diverse and expansive network that will provide you with a wealth of resources, opportunities, and support throughout your career.

The Impact of a Robust Network

A robust network of mentors, peers, and allies can have a profound impact on your career. It provides access to opportunities, guidance, and support that are essential for navigating the complexities of male-dominated industries. By building and maintaining a strong network, you equip yourself with the resources and connections needed to succeed and thrive. Your network becomes not only a source of professional growth but also a community of support that empowers you to achieve your goals and make a lasting impact in your field.

Navigating Office Politics

Navigating office politics can often feel like engaging in an invisible game, where the rules are unwritten and the players are not always obvious or favorable. This dynamic is particularly challenging in male-dominated industries, where decision-making power may be concentrated among a few key individuals. However, understanding and participating in office politics is not about manipulation or deceit—it's about being aware of the power structures, relationships, and unwritten rules that shape workplace decisions.

Successfully navigating these dynamics can be exhausting, but it can also lead to positive outcomes, such as strategic positioning, building influential relationships, and advancing your career without compromising your values. Here's how to better understand the landscape of office politics:

Recognize Power Structures

Every workplace has a power structure—formal or informal—that dictates who holds influence. This structure may not always align with the organizational chart. Some individuals wield significant power due to their roles, tenure, or relationships, even if they don't hold a high-ranking title.

Understanding who these key players are and how they influence decisions is the first step in navigating office politics.

Identify Key Decision-Makers

In any organization, certain individuals or groups are responsible for making important decisions. These decision-makers often have the ear of top leadership and can sway the direction of projects or initiatives. Identifying who these people are and understanding their priorities can help you align your efforts with their goals, increasing your chances of success.

Observe Workplace Dynamics

Pay attention to how people interact, who collaborates with whom, and how conflicts are resolved. Notice the unwritten rules that govern behavior, such as how feedback is given, how meetings are run, or how success is recognized.

Observing these dynamics will give you insights into the workplace culture and help you navigate it more effectively.

Building Strategic Relationships

In any workplace, especially in environments where office politics play a significant role, building strategic relationships is crucial for career advancement and success. These relationships go beyond surface-level networking; it requires cultivating meaningful connections with key individuals who can provide mentorship, guidance, sponsorship or support. Often, these are people who can help you navigate the complexities of your organization. Strategic relationships not only enhance your visibility and access to resources but also position you as a valuable connector within the organization. Here's how to effectively build and leverage strategic relationships:

1. **Cultivate Relationships with Influencers**: Building relationships with those who have influence is a key aspect of navigating office politics. This doesn't mean aligning yourself with power for its own sake, but rather building genuine connections with individuals who can provide mentorship, guidance, or support. These relationships can help you gain visibility, access to resources, and opportunities for collaboration.

2. **Foster Cross-Departmental Alliances**: Don't limit your network to your immediate team or department. Building alliances across different areas of the organization can give you a broader perspective and open up new opportunities. It also positions you as a connector, someone who can bring together diverse perspectives and resources to achieve common goals.

3. **Engage with Gatekeepers**: In many organizations, there are gatekeepers—individuals who control ac-

cess to information, resources, or key decision-makers. Building a positive relationship with these gatekeepers can be crucial, as they often hold the keys to advancing your projects or gaining visibility.

Navigating Conflicts and Challenges

Conflicts and other challenges are an inevitable part of any workplace, especially in environments where office politics are at play. How you navigate these situations can significantly influence your career trajectory. It's essential to approach conflicts with a strategic mindset, balancing diplomacy with assertiveness, and maintaining professionalism under pressure. Successfully managing these dynamics not only preserves your relationships but also positions you as a capable and resilient leader. Here's how to effectively navigate conflicts and challenges in the workplace:

Manage Conflicts Diplomatically

Conflict is inevitable in any workplace, but how you handle it can significantly impact your career. Approach conflicts with a solution-oriented mindset, focusing on resolving the issue rather than winning the argument.

Use diplomacy to navigate disagreements, ensuring that you maintain professional relationships even when opinions differ.

Stay Professional Under Pressure

Office politics can sometimes create high-pressure situations where emotions run high. It's important to remain calm and professional, even in the face of challenges.

Maintaining your composure not only reflects well on you but also helps to de-escalate tense situations and keep discussions productive.

Know When to Stand Your Ground

While diplomacy is important, there are times when you need to stand your ground on issues that align with your values. For me, this has always been particularly challenging because justice ranks so high on my list of core values. It's difficult to step back when I feel like something is unfair or unjust. However, I've learned to ask myself a crucial question before I engage: *What is the purpose of fighting this battle, and what outcome do I hope to achieve?*

Much like I evaluate ROI in business operations, I now consider the ROI of engaging in a particular moment's battle. Is it worth it to me in the long term? What are the potential risks, and can the desired outcome be achieved through a different path, perhaps down the road?It's not just about standing up for what's right—it's about being strategic in how and when you do so. Sometimes, the battle might not be worth the immediate cost which can have a negative impact overall, and there could be other ways to achieve the outcome you desire later on.

Choose your battles wisely, and when you take a stand, ensure that it's for a cause you genuinely believe in and that you've thoughtfully considered the potential consequences. Standing your ground can be powerful when done with intention, foresight, and a clear understanding of what's at stake.

Enhancing Your Visibility

In any workplace, particularly in competitive environments, visibility is key to career advancement. Being recognized for your contributions can open doors to new opportunities and solidify your reputation as a valuable team member. Enhancing your visibility isn't just about self-promotion; it's about strategically positioning yourself as a proactive, collaborative, and effective leader within your organization. Here's how you can effectively enhance your visibility:

· **Take Initiative**: One way to enhance your visibility in a positive way is to take initiative on projects or tasks that align with organizational goals. Volunteering to lead a new project, offering innovative solutions, or proposing new ideas can set you apart as a proactive and valuable team member.

· **Share Credit Generously**: Office politics can sometimes create competition among colleagues, but sharing credit for successes can actually enhance your reputation. When you acknowledge the contributions of others, you build goodwill and strengthen your professional relationships. This collaborative approach can also position you as a leader who values teamwork and collective achievement.

· **Communicate Your Achievements**: While it's important to be humble, it's also essential to ensure that your contributions are recognized. Find appropriate ways to communicate your achievements, whether through regular updates to your manager, during team meetings, or through internal communications channels. Highlighting your successes helps others see the value you bring to the organization and can lead to new opportunities.

Navigating Ethical Dilemmas

You may occasionally face situations that challenge your ethical standards. Navigating these dilemmas requires a strong commitment to your values, as well as the wisdom to know when to seek advice or make difficult decisions. Maintaining your integrity is essential not only for your personal well-being but also for building a reputation as a trustworthy and principled professional.

Maintain Integrity

Office politics can sometimes present ethical dilemmas, where you may feel pressured to compromise your values to get ahead. It's crucial to maintain your integrity in these situations. Always prioritize honesty, transparency, and fairness in your actions. By staying true to your values, you build a reputation for trustworthiness, which is invaluable in the long run.

Seek Guidance When Needed

If you encounter a situation that challenges your ethical standards, don't hesitate to seek guidance from a mentor, trusted colleague, or HR representative. Sometimes, an outside perspective can help you navigate the dilemma while maintaining your professional integrity.

Know When to Walk Away

In some cases, the political dynamics of an organization may become toxic or misaligned with your values. If you find yourself in a situation where navigating office politics consistently requires you to compromise your principles, it may be time to consider other opportunities.

Your well-being and ethical standards should always take precedence over career advancement.

The Benefits of Mastering Office Politics

Mastering office politics doesn't mean engaging in manipulative behavior; rather, it involves understanding the dynamics at play and strategically positioning yourself within them. By effectively navigating office politics, you can build stronger relationships, gain influence, and achieve your career goals. It allows you to contribute more effectively to your organization's success while maintaining your integrity and staying true to your values.

In male-dominated industries, where the political landscape may be particularly complex, these skills are even more critical. By developing a keen awareness of workplace dynamics and using them to your advantage, you empower yourself to advance in your career while fostering a positive and collaborative work environment.

Chapter Three

Advocating for Yourself

In male-dominated industries, advocating for yourself is essential for career growth, personal fulfillment, and maintaining your integrity in the face of challenges. Whether it's negotiating for a raise, pushing for a promotion, handling discrimination, or ensuring your ideas are heard, self-advocacy is about taking ownership of your career and making sure your contributions are recognized.

Preparing yourself with strategies and mindset will help you boldly advocate effectively for yourself while also addressing the critical issue of dealing with discrimination, bias, and misogyny.

Take Control of Your Career

Self-advocacy is about taking proactive steps to shape your career trajectory. In environments where women may be underrepresented and face systemic barriers, it's particularly important to ensure that your accomplishments and ambitions are visible. Advocating for yourself empowers you to steer your career in the direction you want, rather than waiting for opportunities to come to you.

Sofia, a project manager for an engineering team, had always prided herself on her ability to keep projects on track and deliver results. But in a male-dominated environment, she often found her voice overshadowed, especially in high-stakes meetings where key decisions were made.

One day, during a critical project review, Sofia presented a strategy she had developed to address a looming deadline. The plan was solid, backed by data and careful analysis. But as she laid out her proposal, she noticed the room's dynamic shift. Her idea was quickly dismissed by a senior engineer who suggested a different approach. The discussion moved on, and her plan was left on the table, untouched.

Frustrated but determined, Sofia knew she couldn't let this go. After the meeting, she requested a private conversation with the project lead. Calmly but firmly, she explained the merits of her strategy, emphasizing the data that supported her approach. She also pointed out how her contributions had been overlooked in the meeting, addressing the bias head-on without confrontation.

The project lead listened, realizing the value in Sofia's proposal and the importance of giving her ideas the consideration they deserved. He agreed to revisit her strategy in the next meeting and ensure it received the attention it warranted.

At the follow-up meeting, the team implemented Sofia's plan, which ultimately led to the project's success. By advocating for herself, Sofia not only secured the recognition she deserved but also demonstrated her leadership and resilience, reinforcing her role as a key player on the team.

Women in male-dominated industries often encounter stereotypes, bias, and even overt misogyny that can hinder their professional growth. By advocating for yourself, you challenge these negative forces and assert your rightful place in the workplace. It's a way of pushing back against the biases that might otherwise hold you back and making it clear that discrimination and misogyny will not go unchallenged.

Advocating for yourself requires confidence, especially when confronting discrimination or bias. Each time you successfully stand up for your rights or assert your value, you reinforce your belief in your abilities. This confidence, in turn, helps you take on bigger challenges and opportunities, even in the face of adversity.

Negotiating for What You Deserve

Advocating for yourself is a skill just like so many other in your career. It requires intentional practice and often pushing yourself into uncomfortable places. As women are often scolded, we often find ourselves hesitant to stretch ourselves when it comes to negotiating for what we deserve. Whether you're discussing a raise, promotion, or additional resources, effective negotiation requires preparation, confidence, and strategic framing of your request. It's not just about asking for more—it's about positioning your ask in a way that aligns with both your goals and the organization's needs. Here's how to negotiate successfully while ensuring your value is recognized:

Preparing for Negotiation

Effective negotiation begins with preparation. Research industry standards for salaries, benefits, and job roles to understand what you should be asking for. Gather data on your contributions, achievements, and the value you bring to the organization.

This evidence will strengthen your case and give you the confidence to negotiate effectively, even when faced with those that might undervalue your work.

Framing Your Ask

When negotiating, it's important to frame your request in a way that aligns with the organization's goals, while also being mindful of the potential biases you may encounter. Explain how what you're asking for—whether it's a raise, promotion, or additional resources—will benefit the company. Position your request as a mutually beneficial arrangement that supports both your career growth and the organization's success, making it harder to dismiss your case.

Handling Objections

During negotiations, you may encounter objections that stem from biases or discriminatory attitudes. Be prepared to address these concerns calmly and rationally. Have counterarguments ready, and be willing to engage in a constructive dialogue.

If you suspect that bias is influencing the negotiation, don't hesitate to bring this to light, tactfully and professionally, by asking for clarity on how decisions are being made.

Knowing Your Worth

One of the most important aspects of negotiation is knowing your worth and not settling for less than you deserve. If the terms being offered don't meet your expectations or market standards, be prepared to walk away or ask for more. Standing firm on your value is crucial to achieving the outcomes you want.

Asserting Your Ideas

Women's voices are often overlooked, undervalued, or dismissed. Despite making up more than half the planet's population, the workplace is still largely designed by men for men. Asserting your ideas in such settings requires both confidence and strategy. It's crucial to find your voice, support your ideas with data, and navigate interruptions and dismissals with tact. Building alliances with like-minded colleagues can further strengthen your position. Here's how to assert your ideas effectively:

- **Finding Your Voice**: Data shows that women's voices are sometimes overlooked, undervalued, or dismissed. This transcends industry and environments, the truth is, that despite making up more than half the planet's population, the world is designed by men for men. It's important to find your voice and ensure that your ideas are heard. Practice speaking up in meetings, contributing to discussions, and sharing your insights. The more you assert your ideas, the more comfortable and confident you'll become, and the harder it will be for others to ignore or dismiss you.

- **Using Data to Support Your Ideas**: Data can be a powerful tool in advocating for your ideas. When presenting your proposals, back them up with evidence, statistics, and research. This not only strengthens your argument but also demonstrates your thoroughness and expertise, making it more difficult to undermine your contributions.

- **Handling Interruptions and Dismissals Tactfully**: It's not uncommon for women in male-dominated industries to be interrupted or have their ideas dismissed. When this happens, it's important to assert yourself respectfully but firmly. If you're interrupted, calmly say, "I'd like to finish my point." If your idea is dismissed, ask for specific feedback on why and use that information to refine and resubmit your idea if necessary. By handling these situations tactfully, you can challenge the behavior without escalating conflict.

- **Seeking Allies**: Building alliances can help you advocate more effectively for your ideas. Identify colleagues who share your goals or are committed to promoting equity, and seek their support before presenting your ideas in larger forums. Having allies who can back you up during discussions can lend credibility to your proposals and help challenge discriminatory attitudes.

Setting and Maintaining Boundaries

Setting and maintaining boundaries is a crucial skill for anyone, but it is especially important—and challenging—for women in the workplace. Historically, women's boundaries have often been invisible or disregarded, making it difficult to navigate professional and personal spaces without overextending themselves or even being left feeling violated.

Whether it's physically, mentally, or emotionally, establishing clear boundaries is essential not just for your health in the workplace, but also for your overall well-being. Mastering this skill is one of the most important steps you can take to protect your integrity, prevent burnout, and maintain a balanced life. Here's how to set and enforce boundaries effectively:

· **Understanding Your Limits**: Advocating for yourself also means setting and maintaining boundaries. This includes knowing your limits in terms of workload, time commitments, and personal space, and recognizing when biased demands or expectations are being placed on you. Don't hesitate to assert your boundaries in these situations to protect your well-being and professional integrity.

· **Communicating Boundaries Clearly and Assertively**: When setting boundaries, communication is key. Clearly articulate your limits to colleagues, supervisors, and clients, and do so with confidence. For example, if you're being unfairly burdened with tasks that align with assumptions about your role or capabilities, make it clear that the exactly where there is a problem. Setting boundaries helps prevent burnout, protect your mental health, and ensure that you're able to maintain your well-being while pursuing your career goals.

· **Enforcing Boundaries Respectfully**: It's one thing to set boundaries, but it's another to enforce them. If someone crosses a boundary, address it respectfully but firmly. Reiterate your limits and explain why they're important. Enforcing boundaries not only protects your well-being but also signals to others that you will not tolerate the behavior.

Handling Discrimination, Bias, and Misogyny

Handling discrimination, bias, and misogyny in the workplace is a complex and deeply personal challenge. While the strategies outlined here offer a starting point, it's important to acknowledge that every situation is unique, and the environment you're in often dictates how safe or effective it is to address a particular incident.

This list is by no means exhaustive, but it provides some key steps to help you navigate these difficult situations. Remember, you are not alone—there are ways to support yourself and others as you advocate for a more equitable workplace.

Recognizing Discrimination and Bias

The first step in handling discrimination or bias is recognizing it when it occurs. Discrimination can take many forms, from subtle microaggressions to overt acts of misogyny or exclusion. Pay attention to patterns of behavior, decision-making processes, and how you and other women are treated in comparison to male colleagues. Recognizing these issues is the foundation of effective advocacy.

Documenting Incidents

When you experience discrimination, bias, or misogyny, it's important to document these incidents. Keep a record of what happened, when it happened, and who was involved.

This documentation can be crucial if you need to escalate the issue to HR or seek legal advice. It also provides you with concrete evidence to support your claims, making it harder for others to dismiss or downplay your experiences.

Addressing the Issue Directly

If you feel safe and comfortable doing so, consider addressing discriminatory behavior directly with the individual involved. This can be done in a private conversation where you calmly explain how their actions or words were inappropriate and how they affected you.

Sometimes, people may not realize the impact of their behavior, and a direct conversation can lead to positive change. However, if the situation is more severe or if direct confrontation feels unsafe, alternative steps should be taken.

Seeking Support and Reporting Misconduct

Don't hesitate to seek support from trusted colleagues, mentors, or allies if you're dealing with discrimination or bias. They can provide advice, share their own experiences, and help you strategize on how to handle the situation. If the behavior persists or is particularly egregious, consider reporting the misconduct to HR or a relevant authority.

Knowing your rights and the procedures in place at your organization can help you navigate this process more effectively.

Building Resilience in the Face of Discrimination

Dealing with discrimination and bias can be emotionally and mentally taxing. It's important to build resilience by focusing on your long-term goals, seeking support, and practicing self-care.

Remember that the issue lies with the discriminatory attitudes or systems, not with you. Maintaining your confidence and commitment to your career goals will help you persevere and continue advocating for yourself, even in challenging environments.

The Long-Term Impact of Self-Advocacy

Being an advocate for yourself is not just about reaching short-term goals; it's also about laying the groundwork for long-term success and personal principles. By consistently standing up for your needs, ideas, and boundaries, you establish yourself as a confident, capable, and assertive professional. Over time, this reputation will open doors to new opportunities, improve your influence in your organization, and help you achieve the career growth you desire. Women often face additional obstacles in recognition and advancement, making self-advocacy crucial. By taking control of your career, voicing your worth, and speaking out against discrimination and bias, you are taking charge of your own success.

Chapter Four

Leadership and Career Growth

I'll never forget my first meeting with my mentor, an executive at a creative bricks company. I had just been laid off, found a new job, and was juggling what felt like a thousand different things, all while boldly declaring, "I want to be the COO at Disney one day." Ambitious? Absolutely. But as my mentor started digging into my passions and goals, she helped me realize that I needed a more structured approach to my career. I couldn't do everything at once. I had to let go of the panic that maybe my current job wasn't on the right path to becoming a COO. With her guidance, I began focusing on what truly mattered, like writing a book on business operations—because, after all, a COO would know how to do that, right?

As I've climbed the corporate ladder, I've had some incredible sponsors, particularly men who recognized my ability to streamline and create efficiency. Yet, I often found myself pigeonholed into solving specific problems rather than on a clear path to leadership. While I've been able to prove my value, the direct path to becoming a COO wasn't always clear. That's when I realized that, while mentorship is invaluable, career development isn't just about finding the right mentors—it's about taking control of your own journey.

Mentorship is key, but to truly step into leadership roles, especially as a woman, we must intentionally craft our career paths, build resilience, and strategically cultivate leadership qualities, whether through traditional routes or our own unconventional ways.

The Power of Mentorship in Career Development

Throughout my career, mentorship has played a vital role in giving me clarity and an outside perspective during overwhelming moments. One particular session stands out in my memory when my mentor helped me shift my focus away from the immediate stress and uncertainty of my job. At the time, I was consumed with thoughts of how to climb the ladder and become a COO someday. However, my mentor reminded me that true leadership goes beyond titles and promotions; it involves developing qualities that make a leader both inside and outside of work. She helped me realize that my passion for business operations wasn't just for a job; it was also the foundation of my leadership journey. Not only was I improving efficiency in the workplace, but I was also dedicated to uplifting others along the way - a sign of true leadership.

Another pivotal mentorship experience came when I was suddenly moved to a new team. My new manager questioned my "listening skills," and it sent me into a crisis of confidence. I've always considered myself a good listener, but her comment rattled me. Thankfully, I had a career coach at the time who helped me realize that this was just someone else's perception getting into my head. Instead of spiraling, I used this feedback to reflect on areas where I could polish my skills and sharpen my focus. Through that process, I discovered my love for operations and solving business problems, and from there, my career gained new momentum.

Impact of Mentorship

Mentorship offers more than just advice; it provides clarity, focus, and encouragement when you need it most. It can fast-track your career by helping you see the bigger picture and recognize areas of growth. A good mentor doesn't just provide feedback—they help you develop self-awareness by offering an outside perspective that's essential for growth. Through mentorship, I've learned that building self-awareness isn't just about identifying weaknesses—it's about sharpening strengths and seeing how they can drive your long-term career goals.

Mentors offer:

- **Clarity:** They help you focus on what truly matters in your career.

- **Focus:** A mentor can guide you through times of uncertainty, helping you prioritize your energy and efforts.

- **Encouragement:** When self-doubt creeps in, mentors offer the support you need to keep moving forward.

- **Self-awareness:** Sometimes, we're too close to see what we need to work on. A mentor can provide the perspective needed for growth.

The path to leadership for women is often clouded by a lack of representation. We see few women in top positions, making it hard to visualize ourselves there. In professional spaces, we may feel out of place, surrounded by a sea of men in power.

The lack of representation is apparent in board meetings and executive teams, where the majority are men. The few women present may stand out, but they are still outnumbered.

Women in leadership roles are often few and far between, surrounded by a sea of male counterparts. In boardrooms and executive meetings, they may stand out as the lone representative of their gender. Common challenges we may experience:

- **Lack of representation:** Fewer women in leadership roles means fewer role models.

- **Difficulty with self-advocacy:** Asking for what you deserve can feel daunting, especially in male-dominated industries.

- **Feeling unqualified:** Imposter syndrome can cause us to doubt our qualifications, even when we have all the skills and experience we need.

Through mentorship, we can break down these barriers by developing confidence, honing leadership skills, and setting a clear path toward our career goals.

The Managers and The Leaders

When discussing career development and leadership, it's important to distinguish between being a manager and being a leader. While both roles are critical in any organization, they serve different purposes and require different mindsets.

Managers focus on processes, manage people, and ensure the day-to-day efficiency of a team or organization. They are primarily concerned with meeting targets, adhering to timelines, and ensuring that everything runs smoothly. Managers are problem-solvers, ensuring that operations are executed according to plan and addressing challenges as they arise.

Leaders, on the other hand, inspire and influence change. They set the vision for the future and create a culture of innovation and collaboration. Leaders aren't just focused on what is happening today—they're looking ahead, planning for long-term success, and encouraging their teams to think big and embrace change. Leaders foster creativity, promote strategic thinking, and challenge the status quo to ensure that the organization grows and evolves.

Manager	**Leader**
· Focus on operational efficiency.	· Set long-term vision and strategy.
· Manage teams and processes.	· Inspire and influence others to embrace change.
· Solve day-to-day problems.	· Foster innovation and creativity.
· Ensure targets and goals are met within specific constraints.	· Drive cultural shifts and encourage a growth mindset.

Aspiring To Lead

The path to leadership isn't just about managing tasks or teams—it's about defining the future and driving the business toward success. I've always aspired to be a leader who inspires others to innovate and think outside the box. My ultimate goal is to become a COO, a role that would allow me to strategically shape the future of an organization while ensuring operational excellence. This hasn't always been a straightforward path, but I've taken intentional steps to position myself as a future leader in the C-suite.

Transitioning to a leadership role requires more than just completing tasks. It requires qualities like thought leadership, resilience, and adaptability. A leader must be able to anticipate challenges and guide their team through them. They should actively seek out opportunities to solve complex business problems, contribute to strategic decisions within the organization, and drive innovation.

Being a leader is not just about being in a position of authority; it's about recognizing when to take charge and guide your career towards your desired destination. I've had moments where I strayed off my chosen path, but I made the conscious decision to refocus my efforts. I am no longer satisfied with simply "helping out" wherever needed in the business; now, I am determined to take control of my own professional journey. When obstacles arise and threaten to derail your progress, be prepared to redirect your efforts towards your ultimate goals, and make sure to demonstrate the value of staying on track to those in charge.

In my leadership journey, I'm committed to not only excelling in operations but also bringing innovation, resilience, and vision to the table. Being adaptable and thinking strategically is what will get me there, and it's what will keep me grounded as I continue to grow into the leader I aspire to be.

Taking Control of Your Career Path

No one is going to hand you the path to leadership—you have to take control of it yourself. As women, we often wait for recognition or opportunities, but the truth is, we need to be intentional about our career development. We need to actively shape our own trajectories, advocate for ourselves, and seek out the right opportunities to grow.

Intentional Career Development

Taking control of my career was a pivotal moment for me. After facing a series of unexpected turns in my journey, I realized that I couldn't wait for the perfect opportunity to fall into my lap. One of the most intentional steps I took was just starting to write a book on business operations. Not only did this demonstrate thought leadership, but it also showcased my deep understanding of the field and positioned me as an expert—essential qualities for the COO role I'm working toward.

There will be times where your will not go as planned. You may be moved to different teams unexpectedly, face doubts about your skills, and wonder you're even on the right path. But rather than letting those moments define you, you have the power to take ownership. Whether it is actively seeking mentors or finding new ways to showcase your expertise, make the conscious decision to shape your own career. I have learned that leadership is about resilience, adaptability, and focusing on what you can control.

Development Paths

There are traditional, time-tested strategies for professional development that are crucial for women aiming for leadership roles:

- **Professional Development:** Attending leadership courses, obtaining certifications like PMP or MBA, and joining industry-specific networks are all solid foundations for career growth. These certifications validate your skills and help build credibility, but they also expand your network, exposing you to other leaders and mentors.

- **Mentorship and Sponsorship:** Actively seeking out mentors and sponsors can be a game-changer. Mentors offer guidance and advice, while sponsors advocate for you behind closed doors and open up opportunities. Having both in your corner can fast-track your journey to leadership.

- However, there are non-traditional paths that are equally—if not more—important in distinguishing yourself as a leader:

- **Thought Leadership:** One of the most effective ways I've taken control of my career is by positioning myself as a thought leader. Writing articles, giving talks, or, in my case, publishing a book, can elevate your profile in the industry. It demonstrates that you're not just doing the work—you're thinking critically about it and influencing the future of the field.

- **Lateral Moves:** Sometimes, career progression isn't about climbing the ladder—it's about broadening your skill set. I've taken on roles that may not have seemed directly tied to leadership at first, but they gave me the tools I needed to grow. Moving across departments or taking on projects outside your comfort zone can give you a holistic understanding of the business and make you more well-rounded as a leader.

· **Resilience and Adaptability:** Career bumps are inevitable. I've faced moments of uncertainty and change, but the key is staying resilient. Emotional intelligence, grit, and adaptability are crucial for weathering those tough moments. It's not always about making the right move immediately, but about learning, adjusting, and bouncing back stronger.

Find Places to Lead

Leadership isn't confined to your job title. One of the best ways to grow as a leader is to find places where you can serve and make an impact outside of your day-to-day role. For me, that has meant starting a chapter for an organization I'm passionate about or serving in leadership positions within my community.

I've had the privilege of serving as a City Commissioner for the City of Durham (insert Batman joke here—because yes, I so wanted to be *that* Commissioner). I'm passionate about social justice and climate change, which led me to join the Board of Directors for the Ellerbee Creek Watershed Association (ECWA). I also founded and serve as the President for the North Carolina Chapter of Latinas in Tech. These leadership roles not only align with my values but also sharpen my leadership skills.

Serving your community can also serve you—it's a win-win! These roles have expanded my network, strengthened my ability to lead, and reinforced my resilience. So, if you're serious about taking control of your career, don't wait for leadership roles to come to you. Start where you are, and build leadership through the causes and communities you care about.

Taking control of your career isn't about waiting for the perfect opportunity; it's about creating opportunities, cultivating resilience, and finding ways to lead, whether in or outside the workplace. By being intentional and embracing both traditional and unconventional growth strategies, you can steer your career toward the leadership role you aspire to, no matter where you are now.

The Journey to Leadership and the COO Role

Choosing leadership for yourself and committing to that path is an empowering decision, especially when the road ahead isn't always clear. For women, particularly in male-dominated industries, it's crucial to take ownership of your journey and intentionally set your sights on leadership roles. I learned this lesson myself when I decided that I wanted to be a Chief Operating Officer (COO). It wasn't a role I'd initially considered, but after months of career coaching, I realized that this was the direction I wanted to take. However, the moment it truly clicked was during a family trip to Disney.

We had toddlers in tow, and what could have been a stressful experience was seamless. Despite the inevitable hiccups that come with traveling with young kids, Disney managed to deliver an experience that was smooth, enjoyable, and meticulously planned. As a huge Marvel fan, I never thought of myself as a "Disney person," but once the Marvel universe became part of the Disney family, I started to pay attention. What struck me most was Disney's unwavering commitment to customer experience.

Every interaction—whether in a park bathroom or watching *Infinity War* for the 55th time—was designed to be please and delight. Disney's ability to capture its brand values and drive them through every facet of the business made me realize: this is the level of operational excellence I wanted to deliver. That's when I knew the COO role was the right fit for me.

From that moment on, I became laser-focused on strategically cultivating the skills and experiences necessary to step into a COO role. I began honing my ability to manage cross-functional teams, ensuring I could bring together different departments to work toward a common goal. I deepened my understanding of business operations—knowing that, to be a COO, I needed to master the art of not only solving problems but creating systems that ensure those problems never arise in the first place.

For example, one of the most impactful ways I've practiced strategic thinking is by leading projects that required a deep understanding of both the operational aspects and the customer experience. This blend of operational efficiency and customer focus is what makes Disney, and other top companies, so successful. I realized that being a COO isn't just about keeping things running smoothly; it's about driving excellence through every interaction and making sure that each department understands its role in delivering that experience.

I also leaned heavily into managing complex, cross-functional teams. In my roles, I've worked to break down silos and ensure that every part of the business is working toward a unified vision. The ability to manage across functions, whether it's marketing, finance, or operations, is critical for a COO, as it ensures alignment with overall business goals.

Leadership is an Ongoing Journey

Leadership isn't something that begins when you get the title—it's something you demonstrate every day, no matter your position. I may not be in the C-Suite yet, but that doesn't stop me from acting like a leader in everything I do. Leadership is about adding value, inspiring others, and continuously improving how the business operates. I've focused on leading from wherever I am, whether it's driving operational improvements in my current role or mentoring others who are earlier in their careers.

One of the most important lessons I've learned is that you don't have to wait for a title to lead. Leading effectively from any position is about recognizing where you can make an impact and taking ownership of that space. It's about being proactive, showing resilience in the face of challenges, and continually seeking out ways to elevate yourself and your team. Whether its writing a book, heading a cross-functional project, or simply improving day-to-day processes, we hae the power to build the foundation for the leadership role we aspire to.

The journey to becoming a COO is ongoing, and each step I take—whether it's learning more about business operations or developing strategic partnerships—brings me closer to that goal. But more importantly, it's not just about reaching the C-Suite. It's about demonstrating leadership now, ensuring that no matter where I am in my career, I'm adding value and making meaningful contributions. Leadership is a journey, not a destination, and I'm committed to walking that path every day.

Building Leadership Skills

Leadership is an extensive skill set that goes beyond the responsibilities of managing, coaching, or mentoring. While management focuses on overseeing tasks and ensuring that projects are completed, and coaching and mentoring involve guiding others to develop their skills and achieve their potential, leadership encompasses a broader vision. Effective leadership requires the ability to inspire and motivate others, make strategic decisions, and navigate complex situations with confidence.

Unlike management, which is often about maintaining order, leadership is about driving change and fostering a positive environment where teams can thrive. Key leadership skills such as communication, emotional intelligence, decision-making, adaptability, and strategic thinking are essential for creating this environment and guiding an organization toward its long-term goals. These skills enable leaders to not only manage operations but also to lead with vision, empathy, and resilience.

- **Communication Skills**: Effective leaders are skilled communicators. Work on developing clear, concise, and persuasive communication skills. This includes both verbal and written communication, as well as the ability to listen actively and empathetically. Strong communication skills enable you to articulate your vision, inspire your team, and navigate complex situations with confidence.

- **Emotional Intelligence (EQ)**: Emotional intelligence is the ability to understand and manage your own emotions, as well as the emotions of others. Cultivating emotional intelligence is crucial for effective leadership, as it allows you to build strong relationships, manage conflict, and create a positive work environment. Leaders with high EQ are often more successful in motivating their teams and fostering collaboration.

- **Decision-Making and Problem-Solving**: Leaders are often faced with complex decisions and challenges. Developing strong decision-making and problem-solving skills is essential for navigating these situations effectively. Practice making decisions based on data, experience, and intuition, and be willing to take calculated risks when necessary. Additionally, focus on developing your ability to think critically and creatively to find solutions to problems.

- **Adaptability and Resilience**: The ability to adapt to change and bounce back from setbacks is a key characteristic of successful leaders. Cultivate adaptability by being open to new ideas, approaches, and challenges. Build resilience by developing a growth mindset, learning from failures, and maintaining a positive attitude in the face of adversity. Leaders who are adaptable and resilient are better equipped to lead their teams through change and uncertainty.

- **Strategic Thinking**: Leaders must be able to think strategically, understanding the bigger picture and long-term goals of the organization. Work on developing your strategic thinking skills by staying informed about industry trends, analyzing market dynamics, and considering the implications of various decisions. Strategic thinking allows you to make informed decisions that align with the organization's goals and drive its success.

Positioning Yourself for Leadership

Positioning yourself for leadership often requires stepping out of your comfort zone and challenging cultural norms that can hold you back. Many of us have been taught to work hard, keep our heads down, and trust that our efforts will be recognized and rewarded. However, in the real world, especially in competitive work environments dominated by men, this approach is rarely enough. I've rarely seen women promoted solely for doing a great job. We often have to work harder than our male counterparts and, more importantly, we must advocate boldly and loudly for ourselves.

Leadership opportunities aren't just handed out—you have to position yourself as a leader by making your contributions visible, seeking feedback, and aligning yourself with the organization's goals. It's about breaking free from the expectation to stay quiet and instead, actively claiming the recognition and opportunities you deserve.

Jordan had always been a dedicated program manager, but they often worked quietly in the background, focusing on getting the job done without seeking much attention. Despite their consistent performance, Jordan noticed they were rarely considered for leadership opportunities. Realizing they needed to make their contributions more visible, Jordan decided to change their approach.

In meetings, Jordan began sharing their ideas and highlighting team achievements, ensuring their voice was heard. This newfound visibility didn't go unnoticed—colleagues and supervisors started seeing Jordan as a confident and proactive leader. Seeking to improve further, Jordan asked for feedback from their manager and mentor, using their insights to refine their leadership skills and communication.

Understanding that leadership is also about helping others, Jordan took on a mentoring role, guiding junior team members and fostering a collaborative work environment. They also made a point to align their work with the company's broader goals, contributing ideas that supported the organization's long-term strategy.

These efforts paid off. When the role of Strategic Alliance Manager opened up at the software company, Jordan was no longer overlooked. Their increased visibility, commitment to mentoring, and alignment with organizational goals made them the natural choice for the role. By stepping into the spotlight, Jordan successfully advanced their career while helping their team and organization thrive.

1. **Be Visible and Vocal**: Make sure your contributions are recognized by being visible and vocal in your organization. Speak up in meetings, share your ideas, and advocate for your team's achievements. Visibility is key to being considered for leadership roles, as it ensures that decision-makers are aware of your capabilities and potential.

2. **Seek Feedback and Act on It**: Actively seek feedback from colleagues, supervisors, and mentors to identify areas for improvement. Use this feedback to refine your skills, address any weaknesses, and continuously develop as a leader. Demonstrating a willingness to learn and grow is a trait that leaders value and is often rewarded with more opportunities.

3. **Mentor and Support Others**: Leadership is not just about advancing your own career; it's also about helping others succeed. Actively mentor and support colleagues who are looking to grow in their careers. By developing others, you demonstrate your leadership

potential and build a network of allies who will support you as you advance.

4. **Align with Organizational Goals**: Position yourself as a leader by aligning your work with the organization's goals and priorities. Understand the organization's vision and strategic objectives, and find ways to contribute to their achievement. Leaders are often those who can see beyond their immediate responsibilities and work towards the broader success of the organization.

Leading with Integrity and Inclusivity

Leading with integrity and inclusivity is fundamental to effective leadership. Integrity requires a strong moral compass and a commitment to doing what is right, even when faced with difficult decisions. This means being honest, transparent, and ethical in all your dealings. Leaders who are trusted and respected for their integrity are more effective in guiding their teams and gaining the support of others, as they create a foundation of trust and credibility.

Equally important is promoting inclusivity. Encouraging inclusivity is not just about creating a positive environment; it's essential for fostering innovation and driving the organization's success. As a leader, it's crucial to create an environment where diverse perspectives are valued, and everyone feels empowered to contribute. Leading by example, you should advocate for diversity and inclusion, actively working to support the advancement of underrepresented groups. By maintaining integrity and promoting inclusivity, you set the stage for a more dynamic, innovative, and successful organization.

Overcoming Speed Bumps and Setbacks

The road to leadership is rarely smooth. Every career will face its share of challenges, setbacks, and unexpected detours. What defines a great leader isn't just success—it's the ability to bounce back from adversity, learn from mistakes, and keep moving forward with resilience.

Facing Career Setbacks

I've certainly had moments where my career didn't go as planned. One of the most memorable setbacks was when I was suddenly moved to a new team after I had invested considerable time and effort into another department. I was ready for a promotion, but instead, I found myself starting over with a new manager who questioned my abilities. This threw me off balance and made me second-guess my skills. However, rather than letting it derail my progress, I leaned into the challenge. I used it as an opportunity to reflect on my strengths, sharpen my skill set, and prove myself once again.

Building Resilience

Resilience is one of the most critical qualities of leadership. Setbacks can be frustrating and discouraging, but overcoming them builds the kind of strength that helps you handle future challenges with grace. I've found that focusing on long-term goals, rather than getting caught up in the temporary frustration of a setback, has been key to staying on track. It's about maintaining perspective—realizing that every obstacle can be a stepping stone if you approach it with the right mindset.

Maintaining adaptability is equally important. Things won't always go according to plan, and that's okay. The ability to pivot when circumstances change, adjust your approach, and keep going is what separates successful leaders from those who give up. Overcoming setbacks isn't about perfection—it's about learning, growing, and staying resilient.

Advice for Women Facing Challenges

For women in particular, setbacks can feel even more personal or overwhelming, especially in industries where representation is lacking. But remember, every setback can be an opportunity in disguise.

Reframe Setbacks as Learning Opportunities

Instead of viewing a setback as a failure, reframe it as a lesson. What can you learn from the experience? How can you use that knowledge to improve your approach next time? This shift in perspective helps you grow rather than dwell on the negative.

Lean Into Self-Reflection

Take time to reflect on your strengths and areas for growth, but remember that resilience doesn't mean sacrificing your well-being or self-deprecating. Setbacks can force us to reconsider our path, but they also offer an opportunity to set boundaries and protect your energy.

Reflection can lead to valuable insights about where you want to go and how to get there, helping you sharpen your skills while ensuring that you prioritize self-care and maintain balance. Use these moments to refocus without pushing yourself to the point of burnout.

Stay Focused on the Bigger Picture

Obstacles may arise, but they are only temporary. Your ultimate objectives are long-term and worth the stress and anxiety. When faced with difficulties, always remember why you chose to pursue leadership in the first place.

Demonstrating Leadership Before the Title

Leadership isn't something that starts when you get a fancy title. It begins long before you step into an official leadership role, and it's something you can demonstrate every day, regardless of your position. Great leadership is about adding value, inspiring others, and contributing to the growth of the organization. It's about taking ownership of your work and consistently striving to improve, whether you're in an entry-level role or working your way toward the C-suite.

Thought Leadership

One of the ways I've shown leadership throughout my career is by positioning myself as a thought leader, even when I didn't hold an official leadership title. Writing a book on business operations was a strategic move for me—not just to share my expertise, but to demonstrate my ability to think critically and influence the conversation around business operations and leadership. It allowed me to establish myself as a subject matter expert and showcase my passion for streamlining processes and driving efficiency.

Leading strategic initiatives and projects that are not part of your typical job description is a great way to stretch your skills and showcase to your organization. Whether it is spearheading a new cross-functional project or taking the lead on solving a complex business problem, I've always sought out opportunities to show that I can lead, even without the title. Leadership is about stepping up when needed, showing that you can provide solutions, and influencing positive change within your organization.

Ways to Lead From Any Role

Leadership isn't about waiting for the title to give you permission to act like a leader. You can start demonstrating leadership qualities and influence in your current role, no matter what it is. One principle that has guided me throughout my career is the belief that people are everything. This may not be everyone's opinion, but to me, your customers—whether internal or external—are the heartbeat of your success.

Every stakeholder is your personal customer, and if you aim to delight them, not only for the organization but for yourself as a brand, you're going to see results. Here's how you can lead from any role:

- **Take Initiative:** Look for problems that need solving or opportunities for improvement and step up to address them. When you show that you can handle challenges without being asked, you build credibility and demonstrate leadership potential.

- **Empower Others:** Leadership is about lifting others. Even if you're not the official leader, you can empower your colleagues by supporting them, sharing knowledge, and encouraging collaboration. The ability to inspire others is one of the most important traits of a leader.

- **Be Customer-Centric:** Whether you're working with internal teams or external clients, treating every interaction like a chance to delight your customers builds trust and showcases your dedication. When you focus on delivering exceptional experiences, you show that you're thinking strategically about how your role impacts the bigger picture.

Building a Leadership Portfolio

Another key way to demonstrate leadership before holding a formal title is to build a portfolio that showcases your leadership qualities, thought leadership, and the initiatives you've led. This portfolio can be used to highlight the projects you've been involved in, the solutions you've implemented, and the ways you've influenced positive change within your organization.

When I started building my leadership portfolio, I focused on the following:

- **Leading Cross-Functional Projects:** I've worked with multiple teams across different departments to drive strategic initiatives. These projects not only helped me grow my skills but also allowed me to demonstrate my ability to manage and collaborate across functions.

- **Showcasing Thought Leadership:** My book on business operations and the articles I've written show that I'm not only doing the work but thinking critically about the future of business and operations. Thought leadership establishes you as an expert and demonstrates your ability to influence the direction of your field.

- **Driving Efficiency and Innovation:** I've consistently looked for ways to improve processes and drive efficiency within organizations. Whether it's improving workflows, streamlining operations, or implementing new tools, my focus on operational excellence aligns with the long-term goals of any leadership role, particularly the COO position I aspire to.

Leadership isn't defined by the title you hold but by the impact you have. By taking ownership of your work, leading from any role, and building a leadership portfolio that highlights your contributions, you're setting yourself up for future leadership positions. Every project, initiative, and idea is an opportunity to show that you are already the leader you aspire to be.

Owning Your Leadership Journey

As we've explored throughout this guide, leadership isn't something that happens overnight or through luck. It's a combination of mentorship, intentional career development, and the ability to differentiate between managing and leading. Mentorship provides the guidance and feedback needed to navigate challenges, but it's ultimately up to you to take control of your path. Whether it's through building relationships, developing your skills, or showcasing your thought leadership, the journey to leadership starts with intentional decisions. The difference between managing and leading lies in your ability to inspire, influence, and think strategically about the long-term goals of the organization.

The leadership journey is yours to own. Whether you aspire to be a COO, like me, or another leadership position, it's essential to cultivate the qualities that will set you apart—resilience, adaptability, strategic thinking, and self-advocacy. Don't wait for the perfect opportunity to fall into your lap—create your own opportunities. Start today by setting intentional goals, seeking out mentors and sponsors, and positioning yourself as a leader, even if you don't have the title yet. Leadership is about demonstrating your value every day and staying committed to your long-term vision.

Now is the time to take control of your career and embrace your leadership journey. Whether it's starting a new project, building a personal brand, or seeking out mentorship, apply these strategies to cultivate the leadership qualities that will propel you to the next level. Own your path, take bold steps, and start leading today. The journey is yours—make it a powerful one.

Chapter Five

Overcoming Challenges

Whether it's grappling with self-doubt, facing setbacks, or dealing with workplace stress, how you handle challenges can significantly impact your career trajectory. By understanding and overcoming these challenges, you empower yourself to thrive in any environment. Whether you're managing self-doubt, bouncing back from setbacks, building resilience, or finding balance, these strategies will help you navigate your career with confidence and strength.

Understanding and Managing Self-Doubt

Elena had always been a high achiever. She graduated at the top of her class in engineering and quickly secured a job at a well-respected tech company. However, as the only woman on her team, Elena often found herself questioning her abilities. Despite her strong performance, she couldn't shake the feeling that she didn't truly belong—that sooner or later, her colleagues would realize she wasn't as capable as they thought.

These feelings intensified as subtle comments from her coworkers began to chip away at her confidence. When she offered ideas in meetings, they were often met with silence or quickly dismissed, only to be embraced when a male colleague presented the same concept later. When she completed a challenging project ahead of schedule, one of her teammates jokingly asked if she had "finally cracked the code" on her own. Another remarked that she was "lucky" to have landed her role.

Over time, these interactions led Elena to internalize the belief that she was somehow less competent than her peers. She started to avoid taking risks, fearing that any mistake would expose her as a fraud. She worked late nights, pushing herself to do more in an attempt to prove she belonged. But no matter how much she achieved, the self-doubt lingered, gnawing away at her confidence.

One day, after a particularly frustrating meeting where her contributions were once again overlooked, Elena confided in a mentor from another department. She admitted that she was struggling with imposter syndrome and felt like she was constantly trying to prove herself. Her mentor listened carefully and then asked Elena to reflect on her achievements—graduating at the top of her class, successfully leading projects, and receiving positive feedback from clients. He pointed out that these accomplishments were clear evidence of her competence.

Elena's mentor leaned back in his chair, thinking for a moment before speaking. "Elena, I've seen your work. You're talented and more than capable—there's no doubt about that. But I think there's something else going on here. Sometimes, it's not about whether or not we're good enough. It's about the environment we're in and the messages we're constantly receiving."

He paused, letting his words sink in. "I know this place can be tough, especially being the only woman in the room most of the time. It's easy to start doubting yourself when you're not getting the recognition you deserve, or when your ideas are brushed aside. But that doesn't mean you're not capable. It means the environment might be making you feel like you're not."

Elena looked thoughtful, so he continued. "It's not uncommon to feel this way, but I want you to understand that it's not a reflection of your actual abilities. It's more about how this place operates and the pressure that can create. Don't let that make you question your worth. You're here because you've earned it, and you're good at what you do. The doubts, they're more about the environment and the signals you're picking up, not because you're not good enough."

This conversation struck a chord with Elena. For the first time, she began to see that the self-doubt wasn't entirely coming from within—it was being amplified by the environment around her. This realization was the first step in reclaiming her confidence and moving forward with a renewed sense of purpose.

This conversation was a turning point for Elena. She began to see that the self-doubt she was experiencing wasn't a personal failing—it was the result of a work environment that subtly, but persistently, undermined her confidence. She realized that the imposter syndrome she was grappling with was paradoxical; it was actually proof of her capability, as the system around her was attempting to diminish her achievements.

Empowered by this realization, Elena started taking steps to reclaim her confidence. She began keeping a journal of her accomplishments and positive feedback, using it as a tool to counteract the negative thoughts that crept in. She also started challenging the dismissive behavior of her colleagues, calmly but firmly asserting her ideas in meetings. Over time, she found that her voice was being heard more often, and the doubts that once plagued her began to fade.

Elena's journey highlights the insidious nature of imposter syndrome, especially for women in competitive fields. It's a reminder that self-doubt is often a reflection of external factors rather than a true measure of one's abilities. By recognizing this and taking proactive steps to affirm her worth, Elena was able to break free from the imposter syndrome trap and reclaim her confidence and career trajectory.

Imposter syndrome is a term that has gained popularity to describe the feeling of being a fraud despite clear evidence of your competence. A study done by KPMG in 2020 showed that at least 75% of women across all industries experienced imposter syndrome during their career. The very fact that you experience imposter syndrome is paradoxical; it's proof that you are capable and that the system around you is attempting to diminish your achievements. This is more than just a personal shortcoming—it's a symptom of a systemic problem that often undermines the confidence of women.

Allowing feelings of imposter syndrome to consume you can have a significant impact on a career by hindering confidence and self-esteem. It can lead to self-sabotage behaviors such as not speaking up or taking on more work than necessary to prove oneself. Some of the strategies to manage self-doubt are to:

· **Acknowledge Your Achievements**: Regularly reflect on your accomplishments, keeping a record of your successes, positive feedback, and milestones. This tangible evidence can serve as a powerful reminder of your competence when self-doubt creeps in.

· **Challenge Negative Thoughts**: When you catch yourself thinking that you're not good enough or that you don't belong, challenge these thoughts by reminding yourself of your qualifications and the reasons you were hired or promoted.

· **Seek Validation from Within**: While external recognition is important, practice affirming your worth based on your own standards and expectations. Develop a strong internal belief in your abilities.

· **Talk About It**: Discussing imposter syndrome with peers, mentors, or even in professional groups can demystify the feeling and reinforce that it's a common experience, not a reflection of your true capabilities.

Turning Obstacles into Opportunities

Setbacks are a natural part of any career, but they don't have to derail your progress. Instead, view them as opportunities for learning and growth. Every obstacle presents a chance to develop new skills, gain valuable experience, and build resilience.

1. **Analyze the Situation**: Take a step back and objectively assess what went wrong. Identify any factors within your control that contributed to the setback, and consider what you can do differently in the future.

2. **Seek Feedback**: Don't be afraid to ask for feedback from colleagues, mentors, or supervisors. Constructive criticism can provide insights that help you improve and avoid similar setbacks in the future.

3. **Focus on What You Can Control**: Instead of dwelling on what went wrong, focus on what you can do moving forward. Set new goals, make a plan, and take proactive steps to get back on track.

4. **Embrace a Growth Mindset**: Adopt a mindset that views challenges as opportunities to grow rather than as threats to your success. This perspective allows you to see setbacks as a natural part of the learning process.

Building Mental and Emotional Strength

Resilience is the ability to bounce back from adversity, maintain a positive outlook, and keep moving forward despite challenges. In the workplace, especially in male-dominated environments, resilience is essential for navigating tough situations, handling stress, and maintaining your mental and emotional well-being. There are so many resources available to build your undestanding around resilience and it is a deeply personal preference. Here are just a few ways you can build resilience with little investment:

- **Develop a Support Network**: Surround yourself with a community of supportive colleagues, mentors, and peers who can provide encouragement and guidance during tough times.

- **Practice Mindfulness**: Mindfulness techniques, such as meditation or deep breathing, can help you stay grounded and calm in stressful situations. These practices can enhance your ability to manage stress and maintain a positive outlook. Periodic mindfulness breaks throughout the day can be incredibly beneficial.

- **Set Realistic Expectations**: Understand that setbacks and challenges are a normal part of any career. Set realistic expectations for yourself and recognize that perfection is not the goal—progress is.

- **Focus on Self-Care**: Taking care of your physical and mental health is crucial for building resilience. Ensure that you're getting enough sleep, eating well, finding movement, and taking time for activities that recharge you.

The Challenge of Work-Life Balance

In high-pressure situations, it's easy to let work consume your life and cause stress and exhaustion. However, finding a balance is crucial for your overall well-being and long-term success. To effectively manage stress, begin by prioritizing and delegating tasks. Identify the most important items on your to-do list and delegate where possible to avoid feeling overwhelmed.

It's also essential to establish clear boundaries between work and personal life, whether that means setting specific work hours, turning off email notifications after a certain time, or taking regular breaks throughout the day. Utilizing time management techniques such as creating to-do lists, scheduling blocks of time for tasks, or using project management software can help you stay organized and prevent work from taking over your personal life. Make sure to set aside time for activities you enjoy outside of work, such as hobbies or spending time with friends, as these can help you recharge and maintain a positive mindset.

Avoiding Burnout

Burnout, a state of emotional, physical, and mental exhaustion, often results from excessive and prolonged stress. To avoid falling into burnout, it's important first to recognize the warning signs, such as chronic fatigue, irritability, and a lack of motivation. If you notice these symptoms, take immediate action to address them.

Seeking support is also crucial—talk to a manager about your workload, seek advice from a mentor, or consult a mental health professional. Additionally, regularly reevaluating your workload can help prevent burnout. Periodically assess your responsibilities, and if you find yourself consistently overextended, consider reassessing your commitments or negotiating changes that better align with your capacity.

A Positive Outlook

To maintain a positive outlook, it's important to regularly reflect on your accomplishments, both big and small. Celebrating your successes, even in the face of challenges, can help reinforce a positive mindset. Incorporating gratitude into your daily routine is another powerful tool—take time to acknowledge and appreciate the good things in your life and career.

Staying connected with friends, family, and colleagues is also essential, as a supportive network can offer encouragement and perspective when you're feeling down. By focusing on these practices, you empower yourself to thrive in any environment. Whether you're managing self-doubt, bouncing back from setbacks, building resilience, or finding balance, these strategies will help you navigate your career with confidence and positivity.

Chapter Six

Building a Supportive Environment

In male-dominated industries, building a supportive environment is not just beneficial—it's essential. Women often face unique challenges that can be difficult to navigate alone. By supporting each other through mentorship, advocacy, and community, we can collectively overcome these obstacles and create a more inclusive and equitable workplace. This chapter explores the importance of lifting up other women and how doing so can lead to stronger, more resilient careers for everyone involved.

The Power of Mentorship

Mentorship is one of the most powerful tools for professional growth, especially for women who may lack representation in leadership roles. A mentor provides guidance, shares valuable insights, and offers support as you navigate your career. For women, having a mentor who understands the specific challenges you face can be incredibly empowering. It's not just about learning the ropes; it's about having someone who believes in your potential and helps you see the possibilities ahead.

Being a mentor is equally important. As you advance in your career, consider how you can support other women coming up behind you. Sharing your experiences, offering advice, and providing encouragement can make a significant difference in someone else's journey. Mentorship is a two-way street—both the mentor and mentee benefit from the relationship, learning and growing together.

Advocating for One Another

Advocacy goes hand in hand with mentorship but extends beyond one-on-one relationships. Advocacy involves actively supporting other women in your organization by speaking up for them, recommending them for opportunities, and ensuring their contributions are recognized. In many workplaces, women's accomplishments are often overlooked or undervalued. By advocating for each other, we can help to break this cycle.

Being an advocate means using your voice and influence to ensure that women's work is seen and valued. It's about challenging biases, addressing inequalities, and creating a culture where everyone has the opportunity to succeed. Advocacy can take many forms, from publicly praising a colleague's work to pushing for more inclusive policies that benefit all employees.

Fostering a Community of Support

Community is the foundation of a supportive environment. When women come together to share their experiences, challenges, and successes, they create a network of support that strengthens everyone involved. This sense of community helps to reduce feelings of isolation, build confidence, and inspire action.

Creating and participating in communities—whether through formal groups, informal networks, or online platforms—allows women to connect with others who share their experiences and goals. These communities provide a safe space to discuss challenges, seek advice, and celebrate victories. They also serve as a powerful collective voice that can advocate for change within the organization and beyond.

The Ripple Effect of Support

Supporting other women doesn't just benefit those directly involved—it has a ripple effect that can transform entire organizations. When women mentor, advocate for, and build communities with each other, they contribute to a culture of inclusivity and collaboration. This culture not only helps individual women succeed but also makes the organization stronger, more innovative, and better equipped to navigate the challenges of the future.

By supporting each other, we can create a workplace where all women feel empowered to pursue their goals, take on leadership roles, and make meaningful contributions. Building a supportive environment isn't just about helping ourselves; it's about paving the way for future generations of women to thrive in their careers.

Strategies for Promoting Inclusivity and Equality in the Workplace

Promoting inclusivity and equality in the workplace isn't just a matter of ethics—it's a strategic business imperative that drives innovation, improves decision-making, and enhances organizational performance. A diverse and inclusive environment brings together a variety of perspectives, experiences, and ideas, leading to more creative solutions and better outcomes.

Championing diversity from a business perspective involves leveraging diverse perspectives for innovation, building teams that reflect the market, encouraging inclusive decision-making, addressing bias in processes, measuring progress, and fostering a culture of respect and inclusion. These strategies, that you can apply directly in your role, not only promote equality but also contribute directly to the success and competitiveness of your organization.

Leverage Diverse Perspectives for Innovation

One of the most significant benefits of a diverse workforce is the wealth of perspectives it brings. When people from different backgrounds, cultures, and experiences collaborate, they approach problems from unique angles, leading to innovative solutions that might not emerge in a more homogenous group. To harness this potential, actively seek out and encourage contributions from all members of your team, especially those whose voices might not always be the loudest.

For example, when tackling a complex project or brainstorming new ideas, make it a point to involve individuals from various departments, experience levels, and backgrounds. Encourage open dialogue and ensure that everyone has the opportunity to share their thoughts. By fostering an environment where diverse perspectives are valued, you'll not only enhance creativity but also improve the quality of the solutions your team produces.

Build Teams That Reflect the Market

Your customers and clients are diverse, so your teams should be too. By building teams that reflect the diversity of your market, you're more likely to understand and meet the needs of a broader audience. This approach can lead to better customer insights, more effective marketing strategies, and ultimately, increased customer satisfaction and loyalty.

When assembling teams or hiring new talent, consider how different perspectives can contribute to understanding and serving your market more effectively. This isn't about ticking boxes; it's about strategically selecting team members who bring valuable insights into the needs, preferences, and behaviors of diverse customer segments. A team that reflects the market is better positioned to create products, services, and marketing campaigns that resonate with a wide range of customers.

Encourage Inclusive Decision-Making

In many organizations, important decisions are often made by a small, homogenous group of leaders. This can lead to blind spots and missed opportunities. To promote inclusivity and equality in decision-making, make it a priority to involve a broader range of voices in the process.

When decisions need to be made, particularly those that will impact the entire organization or customer base, ensure that the decision-making group includes individuals with diverse perspectives. This could involve inviting team members from different departments, levels of seniority, or cultural backgrounds to participate in discussions. By widening the circle of decision-makers, you're more likely to consider all relevant factors and make choices that benefit the entire organization.

Address and Overcome Bias in Processes

Bias, whether conscious or unconscious, can have a significant impact on hiring, promotions, and other workplace processes. To champion diversity effectively, it's essential to recognize and address these biases. Start by critically evaluating the processes in place at your organization. Are there patterns that suggest certain groups are consistently favored or overlooked? Are there steps in the hiring or promotion process that could be unintentionally excluding qualified candidates?

Implementing structured, objective criteria for evaluating candidates and performance can help reduce bias. For example, standardizing interview questions and using diverse panels for hiring decisions can help ensure that all candidates are evaluated fairly. Additionally, regularly reviewing and updating these processes can help identify and correct any biases that may have been overlooked.

Measure and Track Progress

To ensure that your efforts to promote inclusivity and equality are effective, it's important to measure and track progress. Set clear, measurable goals related to diversity within your team or organization, and regularly assess how well you're meeting them. This could involve tracking the diversity of new hires, monitoring the career progression of employees from underrepresented groups, or measuring the inclusivity of your team's culture through employee feedback.

By keeping a close eye on these metrics, you can identify areas where more work is needed and make informed decisions about where to focus your efforts. Additionally, sharing these results with your team and leadership can help build accountability and ensure that diversity remains a priority within the organization.

Create a Culture of Respect and Inclusion

Promoting diversity isn't just about bringing different people together—it's about creating a culture where everyone feels respected, valued, and included. This means fostering an environment where all employees feel safe to express their ideas, share their experiences, and contribute to their fullest potential.

Encourage behaviors that promote respect and inclusion, such as active listening, empathy, and open-mindedness. Address any instances of exclusion or disrespect immediately, and make it clear that such behaviors are not tolerated. By creating a culture of respect, you not only enhance the well-being of your employees but also strengthen the overall effectiveness and cohesion of your team.

Engaging Allies and Being an Agent of Transformation

Creating meaningful change within an organization, especially regarding gender equity, requires more than just individual effort; it demands collective action. As an agent of change, your role is not only to advocate for gender equity but also to engage others—especially male colleagues and leaders—in this important conversation. Allies are crucial in this journey, as they not only support and amplify your efforts but can also act as sponsors, representing and advocating for you when you're not in the room.

Engaging Allies for Greater Impact

Allies play a pivotal role in driving change within an organization. When male colleagues and leaders become allies, they help bridge the gap between different perspectives and contribute to creating a more inclusive environment. To engage potential allies, start by educating them on the importance of gender equity—not just as a moral issue, but as a business imperative that leads to better decision-making, innovation, and overall success.

Open dialogue is key. Initiate conversations with male colleagues about the challenges women face in the workplace, and explain how they can help address these issues. Encourage them to listen, learn, and participate in efforts to promote equity. By involving them in discussions and initiatives, you help create a shared sense of responsibility and commitment to change.

Building a Network of Sponsors

Allies can also serve as powerful sponsors—individuals who not only support your career but actively advocate for your advancement. Sponsors use their influence to recommend you for opportunities, highlight your achievements, and ensure your voice is heard in decision-making processes. Building a network of sponsors involves identifying key leaders within your organization who can champion your cause.

To cultivate these relationships, demonstrate your value by consistently delivering high-quality work and showing leadership potential. Engage with potential sponsors by seeking their advice, sharing your career goals, and asking for their support in specific areas. Sponsors are more likely to advocate for you when they understand your ambitions and see the impact you're making.

Leading the Charge for Organizational Change

As an agent of change, it's important to take proactive steps to foster a more equitable workplace. This involves not only advocating for yourself and other women but also creating structures and initiatives that promote lasting change. Consider starting or leading diversity and inclusion initiatives, mentoring programs, or workshops that focus on gender equity and leadership development.

By positioning yourself as a leader in these efforts, you set an example for others to follow and create a ripple effect that can transform the organization's culture. When allies and sponsors join you in these initiatives, the impact is amplified, leading to more significant and sustainable change.

Creating a Culture of Accountability

Change doesn't happen overnight, and it requires ongoing effort and accountability. Engage your allies and sponsors in establishing measurable goals for gender equity and regularly review progress toward these goals. Encourage them to use their influence to hold the organization accountable for creating an inclusive environment where everyone can thrive.

By working together with allies and sponsors, you can drive meaningful change within your organization, ensuring that gender equity is not just a conversation but a reality. Your efforts, combined with the support of those who champion your cause, will help create a workplace where diversity is valued, equity is achieved, and everyone has the opportunity to succeed.

A Personal Board of Directors

If you own a business, or work in an organization, you undoubtedly have some familiarity with the function of your company's Board of Directors. Investopedia describes a "board of directors (BofD) is the governing body of a company, whose members are elected by shareholders (in the case of public companies) to set strategy, oversee management, and protect the interests of shareholders and stakeholders.

Just like a company's board of directors, your personal board is a curated group of individuals who bring different experiences, skills, and insights to the table. These can include mentors, peers, industry experts, and even trusted colleagues. The purpose of this board is to offer you a well-rounded source of advice and feedback as you face decisions and challenges in your professional life.

As you face multifaceted challenges, from navigating office politics to overcoming biases. Having a personal board of directors provides you with a sounding board for these issues, helping you to see things from multiple angles and make informed decisions. Each member of your board offers unique expertise that can help you strategize, problem-solve, and ultimately advance in your career.

As Sarah walked across the stage to receive her Bachelor's degree, she felt a mix of excitement and anxiety. Graduating with a degree in marketing, she was about to start a summer internship at a prestigious advertising agency—an opportunity she knew could open doors to her dream job. But she also knew that entering the professional world was a whole new challenge. To succeed, she would need more than just her education; she would need guidance, support, and a network of people who could help her navigate this new chapter of her life.

During one of her final classes, a professor had mentioned the idea of building a personal board of directors—a group of mentors and advisors who could provide guidance and support throughout her career. Inspired by this idea, Sarah decided to start building her own board before she even set foot in her new internship.

Her first step was reaching out to her professor, Dr. Martinez, who had always been supportive and provided valuable insights throughout her college years. Sarah admired Dr. Martinez's career trajectory and her ability to balance academic excellence with real-world industry experience. When Sarah asked if she would be willing to serve as a mentor, Dr. Martinez was thrilled and agreed without hesitation.

Next, Sarah thought about her network outside of college. During a networking event a few months earlier, she had connected with Lisa, a senior marketing manager at another agency. They had hit it off, and Lisa had offered to stay in touch. Sarah reached out to Lisa, explaining her desire to build a personal board of directors and asking if she could be part of it. Lisa was impressed by Sarah's initiative and agreed to offer her support and advice.

Sarah also knew that she needed someone who was closer to her own experience—someone who had recently made the transition from college to the professional world. She thought of Emily, a recent graduate who had completed the same internship the year before and had successfully landed a full-time position at the agency. Emily had been open about her journey on social media, sharing tips and advice for new graduates entering the workforce. Sarah reached out to Emily and asked if she could share her experiences and offer guidance. Emily was more than happy to help, remembering how valuable it had been to have support during her own transition.

With Dr. Martinez, Lisa, and Emily on her personal board of directors, Sarah felt more confident as she started her internship. She met with each of them regularly—Dr. Martinez provided strategic career advice and helped her think long-term; Lisa offered insights into the industry and tips for making a strong impression during her internship; and Emily gave her practical advice on how to navigate the day-to-day challenges of being a new professional.

Throughout the summer, Sarah encountered various challenges—tight deadlines, navigating office politics, and managing her workload—but she never felt alone. Whenever she faced a difficult situation, she turned to her board of directors for guidance. They helped her see things from different perspectives and provided the encouragement she needed to keep pushing forward.

As the internship drew to a close, Sarah was offered a full-time position at the agency, a testament to her hard work, determination, and the support she had received from her personal board of directors. She knew that this was just the beginning of her career journey, but with her board by her side, she felt ready to take on whatever came next.

Sarah's story is a powerful example of how building a personal board of directors can provide young professionals with the support, guidance, and confidence they need to transition from college to the workforce and achieve their career goals. By surrounding herself with trusted mentors and advisors, Sarah was able to navigate the challenges of her internship, secure a full-time job, and lay the foundation for a successful career.

Build Your Board

Start by identifying people whose judgment you trust and who have different strengths that complement your own. This might include a mentor who has walked a similar path, a peer who can offer candid feedback, or an industry leader whose experience you admire. It's important to have a mix of individuals who can provide both professional and personal guidance.

Once you've identified potential members, approach them with clear intentions. Let them know why you value their input and how you see their role in your personal board of directors. Be specific about the kind of support and advice you're seeking. This transparency sets the tone for a productive and meaningful relationship.

Engaging with Your Board

Regular communication is key to maintaining an effective personal board of directors. Schedule periodic check-ins with each member to discuss your progress, challenges, and goals. These conversations can be formal or informal, depending on your relationship with each board member. The goal is to keep them informed and engaged so they can provide timely and relevant advice.

Don't forget to express your gratitude and to also offer your support in return. A personal board of directors is a two-way street, where both parties can benefit from the exchange of ideas and experiences.

The Benefits of a Personal Board

By assembling your own personal board of directors, you're not just gaining access to a diverse range of perspectives—you're also building a safety net of support that can help you navigate the complexities of your career. This board becomes an invaluable resource, offering you guidance, boosting your confidence, and helping you to stay aligned with your long-term goals.

In male-dominated industries, where the path to success can be particularly challenging, having a strong support system can make all the difference. It is like a shield of armor, empowering you to take bold risks and lead with unwavering confidence. With a personal board of directors by your side, you have a team of trusted advisors who will always have your back. This added layer of support creates an even stronger foundation for navigating the hurdles and obstacles faced in male-dominated industries. With the guidance and counsel of your personal board, you can persevere and achieve your professional goals with determination and resilience.

Chapter Seven

Embracing Your Own Journey

As you navigate your career it's essential to take ownership of your path and embrace the challenges that come your way. These challenges, while daunting, are also opportunities for growth, resilience, and leadership. By advocating for yourself, supporting others, and continuously developing your skills, you position yourself not only to succeed but to thrive. Remember, your journey is uniquely yours—take pride in the strides you make, and never shy away from stepping into the spotlight. Your contributions are valuable, and your success is well-deserved.

The Future of Women in Male-Dominated Industries

Alejandra leaned against the rail outside the White House, gazing up at its iconic facade that gleamed in the afternoon sun. The weight of her family's hopes seemed to press just as heavily against her chest as her ID badge against her blazer. She let out a long breath that had been held in too long—each exhalation releasing fragments of doubt that dared to cloud her purpose.

She walked forward to stand alone on stage set in the garden, bathed in a spotlight that seemed to carve out space just for her amidst a sea of suits and ties. With every word delivered with clarity and confidence, she claimed this space—her space—in an place where few shared her story or bore her resemblance. Yet here she was: not just filling a role but reshaping it entirely.

The landscape for women across industries is changing, and the future holds immense promise. As more women step into leadership roles and more organizations recognize the value of diversity, the barriers that once seemed insurmountable are beginning to crumble. Women are increasingly seen not just as participants in these industries but as drivers of innovation, change, and success. The collective efforts of women who advocate for themselves and each other are reshaping workplaces, making them more inclusive, dynamic, and equitable.

The role women will play in this evolving landscape is crucial. By continuing to break barriers, mentor the next generation, and push for systemic change, women will redefine what leadership looks like across industries. The journey may not always be easy, but it is one filled with potential and purpose. The future is bright, and women are at the forefront of this transformation.

Call to Action

Now, it's time to put what you've learned into action. Apply the strategies, insights, and lessons from this guide to your own career. Advocate boldly for yourself, seek out leadership opportunities, and build a network of mentors, allies, and sponsors who will support you along the way. But don't stop there—be a champion for other women, too. Share your knowledge, offer mentorship, and create spaces where women can connect, support, and uplift one another. By doing so, you contribute to a stronger, more inclusive environment for everyone.

Your journey is part of a larger movement toward equity and excellence in the workplace. Embrace it, own it, and help shape the future for women in your industry. Together, we can create a world where everyone has the opportunity to thrive.

Chapter Eight

Practical Tools and Resources

WWW.LATINABYTES.COM

For personalized tools, resources, and recommended readings tailored to help women and underrepresented groups navigate and thrive in your career no matter what industry you're in, visit my website. Here, you'll find a curated selection of content designed to empower you on your professional journey and provide the support you need to succeed.

Recommended reading to continue your journey

Invisible Women: Data Bias in a World Designed for Men by Caroline Criado Perez

An eye-opening exploration of how the world is often built without considering women's needs, highlighting the importance of data in creating equitable systems.

Crucial Accountability: Tools for Resolving Violated Expectations, Broken Commitments, and Bad Behavior, Second Edition by Kerry Patterson , Joseph Grenny, Ron McMillan , Al Switzler (Author), David Maxfield

Crucial Accountability highlights the importance of addressing broken promises, missed deadlines, and poor behavior, which accounts for the majority of relationship breakdowns. This book provides practical tools for tackling these issues in a way that not only solves the immediate problem but also strengthens relationships.

Set Boundaries by Nedra Glover Tawib

Offers practical advice on how to establish healthy boundaries in all areas of life, helping readers improve their relationships, reduce stress, and prioritize self-care. Tawwab emphasizes the importance of clear communication and setting limits as essential steps to creating peace in one's life.

Break the Good Girl Myth by Majo Moline

Explores the social conditioning that encourages women to conform to outdated and limiting expectations. Molfino identifies five "Good Girl" myths and offers actionable steps to break free from these patterns, empowering women to embrace their true potential and live more authentically.

The Memo: What Women of Color Need to Know to Secure a Seat at the Table by Minda Harts

A powerful guide for women of color navigating their careers, offering advice on overcoming obstacles, building networks, and achieving success in the workplace.

More Than Enough: Claiming Space for Who You Are (No Matter What They Say) by Elaine Welteroth
A memoir and motivational guide that explores Elaine Welteroth's journey as a Black woman in media and how she navigated and redefined leadership roles.

Professional Troublemaker: The Fear-Fighter Manual by Luvvie Ajayi Jones
A humorous and inspiring guide on how to fight fear and embrace courage, especially for women of color seeking to break barriers in their careers.

Real Life by Brandon Taylor
A novel that follows Wallace, a Black gay student in a predominantly white Midwestern university, exploring themes of alienation, race, and sexuality with sharp psychological insight.

Brown Girl, Brownstones by Paule Marshall
A coming-of-age novel that explores the experiences of a young Barbadian girl growing up in Brooklyn, touching on themes of identity, race, and ambition.

Me and White Supremacy by Layla Saad

A guide designed to help readers understand and dismantle internalized white supremacy. Through a series of reflective exercises, Saad encourages readers to confront their own biases, privilege, and complicity in upholding racism, offering a path toward anti-racist action and allyship.

Mediocre: The Dangerous Legacy of White Male America by Ijeoma Oluo

Examines the historical and systemic ways white male dominance has shaped American society. Oluo explores how this legacy perpetuates inequality and harms marginalized communities, while also addressing how this power structure hinders social progress and justice. The book calls for a reevaluation of leadership and power in America.

First Gen: A Memoir by Alejandra Campoverdi
Alejandra Campoverdi's First Gen is a compelling memoir that delves into the complexities of being a "First and Only," offering a candid exploration of her journey as a Mexican American woman navigating the extremes of life—from growing up on welfare to serving as a White House aide—while grappling with the sacrifices and contradictions that come with pursuing the American Dream.

Support Networks and Organizations

Building a strong support network is vital for personal and professional growth, especially in challenging environments like male-dominated industries. While there are many organizations and networks available, the key is to seek out those that resonate with your unique interests, values, and experiences. Whether you are looking for mentorship, advocacy, or a community of peers who share your goals, finding the right support network can make a significant difference in your journey.

Consider what aspects of your identity, career, and interests are most important to you—whether it's your professional field, cultural background, gender identity, or a combination of these factors. There are networks and organizations designed to support individuals at various intersections, offering resources, connections, and opportunities tailored to your specific needs.

Explore different options, attend events, and engage with communities that align with your aspirations. These networks can provide invaluable support, whether it's through professional development programs, networking opportunities, or simply offering a space where you can connect with others who understand your experiences. By actively seeking out and participating in these organizations, you not only gain the support you need but also contribute to a broader community that is working toward greater inclusivity and equity in the workplace.

Remember, the strength of your support network is not just about the resources it offers—it's about the relationships you build and the empowerment you gain from being part of a community that champions your growth and success.

Checklist:
Strategies for
Women to Succeed

Checklist: Practical Strategies for Women to Succeed in Male-Dominated Fields

Build a Strong Personal Brand

- [ ] **Develop a clear and confident self-presentation**: Reflect on your strengths, values, and what makes you unique in your field.
- [ ] **Craft an elevator pitch**: Summarize who you are, what you do, and why it matters in 30 seconds or less.
- [ ] **Showcase your achievements**: Regularly update your resume, LinkedIn profile, and portfolio with your accomplishments.

Cultivate a Support Network

- [ ] **Join professional organizations**: Look for groups that support women in your industry.
- [ ] **Find a mentor**: Seek out experienced professionals who can provide guidance and advice.
- [ ] **Build peer connections**: Develop relationships with colleagues at all levels to create a support system.

Enhance Your Skills

- [ ] **Pursue continuous learning**: Stay updated on industry trends, tools, and technologies through courses, workshops, and certifications.
- [ ] **Develop leadership skills**: Focus on areas such as decision-making, team management, and communication.
- [ ] **Seek feedback**: Regularly ask for constructive criticism from peers and supervisors to improve your performance.

Advocate for Yourself

- [ ] **Negotiate confidently**: Be prepared to negotiate for salary, promotions, and opportunities that align with your career goals.
- [ ] **Set clear boundaries**: Define and communicate your limits to maintain a healthy work-life balance.
- [ ] **Voice your ideas**: Actively participate in meetings and discussions, ensuring your ideas are heard and considered.

Navigate Office Politics

- ☐ **Understand the dynamics**: Observe and learn the unspoken rules, key players, and power structures in your workplace.
- ☐ **Build alliances**: Collaborate with colleagues across departments to strengthen your influence and visibility.
- ☐ **Stay professional**: Maintain integrity, respect, and professionalism in all interactions, even in challenging situations.

Manage Imposter Syndrome

- ☐ **Acknowledge your achievements**: Keep a record of your successes to remind yourself of your capabilities.
- ☐ **Challenge negative thoughts**: Replace self-doubt with positive affirmations and realistic assessments of your skills.
- ☐ **Seek support**: Talk to mentors or peers about your feelings and gain perspective from their experiences.

Embrace Resilience and Adaptability

- ☐ **Learn from setbacks**: View challenges as opportunities for growth and development.
- ☐ **Stay adaptable**: Be open to change and willing to adjust your strategies to align with evolving industry demands.
- ☐ **Celebrate progress**: Recognize and celebrate your milestones, no matter how small, to stay motivated.

Promote Inclusivity

- ☐ **Support other women**: Mentor, advocate for, and collaborate with other women in your field.
- ☐ **Champion diversity**: Advocate for policies and practices that promote inclusivity and equality in the workplace.
- ☐ **Lead by example**: Demonstrate inclusive leadership by fostering a collaborative and respectful work environment.

Prioritize Self-Care

- ☐ **Practice stress management**: Incorporate techniques such as mindfulness, exercise, and hobbies into your routine.
- ☐ **Maintain work-life balance**: Set boundaries to ensure you have time for rest, relaxation, and personal pursuits.
- ☐ **Seek help when needed**: Don't hesitate to reach out for professional support, whether through therapy, coaching, or other resources.

Plan Your Career Path

- ☐ **Set long-term goals**: Define your career aspirations and create a roadmap to achieve them.
- ☐ **Identify opportunities for advancement**: Look for roles, projects, or initiatives that align with your goals and offer growth potential.
- ☐ **Review and adjust regularly**: Revisit your goals and strategies periodically to ensure they remain aligned with your evolving career trajectory.

Worksheet: Salary Negotiation

Salary Negotiation Worksheet

This worksheet is designed to empower you as you prepare for salary negotiations by helping you build a strong business case rooted in clear objectives, strategic thinking, and effective communication. Whether you're negotiating for a raise, a promotion, or better working conditions, this tool guides you through identifying your interests, understanding your employer's perspective, and crafting a compelling argument that aligns your goals with the company's needs.

By leveraging tactics inspired by "Never Split the Difference" and addressing challenges unique to women in the workplace, this worksheet equips you with the confidence and preparation necessary to advocate for what you deserve. Use it to structure your thoughts, anticipate objections, and develop a negotiation strategy that leads to a successful outcome.

Parties Involved

Parties	Roles / Positions	Influence
Yourself	Your Role in the organization	What leverage or influence do you hold?
Hiring Manager or HR	Who will you be negotiating with?	What is their role and decision-making power?
Potential Allies	Colleagues, mentors, or sponsors who support your case.	How can they support your negotiation?

Interests

Your Interests

Why are you negotiating?

Example: Fair compensation, career growth, work-life balance.

Employer's Interests

What are your employer's goals?

Example: Retaining top talent, aligning salaries with market rates.

Shared Interests

What do both parties want?

Example: Long-term success for both you and the company.

Objectives

Your Objectives

What are your specific goals?

Example: Secure a 10% salary increase, additional benefits, or flexible working conditions.

Employer's Objectives

What might your employer be aiming for?

Example: Minimize costs while maintaining employee satisfaction.

Mutual Objectives

What common ground can you find?

Example: A compensation package that motivates you while fitting within the company's budget.

Value Proposition

What You Bring to the Table

List your unique skills, achievements, and contributions.

Example: Led a project that increased revenue by 15%

How It Benefits the Company

Connect these to the company's success and goals.

Example: Your leadership directly contributes to the company's growth.

Potential Objections & Counter-Strategies

Potential Objections

Identify objections your employer might raise (e.g., budget constraints).

Example: "We can't afford a raise right now.

Your Counter-Strategies

Prepare your responses and alternatives (e.g., negotiate for additional benefits or a phased increase).

Example: "Given my contributions, can we explore a phased increase or additional benefits like stock options or professional development opportunities?

Tactics to Handle Objections

Tactics	How to use them
Mirroring: Repeat the last few words your employer says to build rapport.	Use it to show you're listening and to encourage them to provide more information.
Labeling: Identify and verbalize the employer's emotions or concerns.	Example: "It seems like the budget is a big concern for you."
Accusation Audit: Acknowledge any concerns they might have before they bring them up.	Example: "You might think I'm just focused on the salary, but I'm really committed to contributing to the company's growth."
Anchoring: Set the tone by being the first to make an offer.	Example: "Given my market research and contributions, I believe a 10% increase is fair."
Calibrated Questions: Ask questions that can't be answered with a simple yes or no.	Example: "How can we find a solution that works for both of us?"

The Negotiation

Mutual Objective

Define the common goal of the negotiation.

Example: A fair and motivating compensation package.

Issues to Negotiate

List the key points you need to discuss (e.g., salary, benefits, work conditions).

Example: Base salary, performance bonuses, stock options.

Issues that Best Connect to Interests

Identify which issues are most important to both you and your employer.

Example: Aligning salary with market rates while ensuring you feel valued and motivated

Final Preparation

Prepare your key points and evidence

Summarize your main arguments and supporting data.

Plan your opening statement and negotiation strategy

Think about how you'll start the conversation and what tactics you'll use.

Know Your Worth

Source and research market rates for your role and be confident in your value

https://www.onetonline.org:

https://www.bls.gov/oes:

https://www.glassdoor.com:

Levels.fyi:

Similar jobs listed on LinkedIn:

Seek Allies

Are there mentors or sponsors who can advocate for you during or after the negotiation?

Practice

Who is a trusted trusted colleague or mentor you can rehearse your negotiation with to refine your approach.

Schedule the meeting

Set a time that allows for a focused and unhurried discussion.

Worksheet: Networking Strategy

Networking Strategy Worksheet

LatinaBytes.com

This Networking Strategy helps you identify and connect with key contacts in your field. It provides a structured approach to networking by helping you list potential events, identify key contacts, and create strategies for building meaningful professional relationships.
This Networking Strategy Worksheet will help you build meaningful connections in your field, providing the foundation for long-term career growth and opportunities. Remember, networking is a continuous process, and these strategies will help you stay proactive and intentional in expanding your professional network.

Potential Networking Events

List upcoming events, conferences, seminars, or meetups relevant to your field where you can connect with industry professionals.

Event	Date	Location/Virtual	Why Attend?

Key Industry Contacts

Identify individuals in your industry who you'd like to connect with. This could include peers, potential mentors, or leaders in your field.

Contact Name	Role/Company	Reason to Connect	Action Plan

Networking Strategy Worksheet

LatinaBytes.com

Strategies for Building Relationships

Outline how you will establish and maintain relationships with your key contacts.

Strategy	Details/Action Plan	Target Date
Follow-Up Emails Send personalized emails following networking events or introductions.		
Social Media Engagement Connect on LinkedIn or Twitter, and engage with their content regularly.		
Informational Interviews Schedule brief meetings to learn more about their work and share your interests.		
Offer Value Share resources, articles, or industry insights that could be useful to your contacts.		
Attend Regular Industry Events Commit to attending key industry events to maintain visibility and grow connections.		

Long-Term Networking Goals

Set specific, measurable goals for your networking efforts. What do you want to achieve through these relationships?

Goal	Target Date	Success Measure

Networking Strategy Worksheet

Progress

Track your networking activities and assess how they're contributing to your career development.

Date	Action(s) Taken	Results/Feedback	Next Step(s)

Worksheet: Building Your Board of Directors

Build Your Board of Directors
www.latinabytes.com

Self-Assessment: Identifying Your Needs

Goals and Challenges:
List your current career goals and any specific challenges you're facing
Example: "I want to transition into a leadership role, but I'm struggling with strategic thinking and networking."

Areas for Growth:
Identify the skills or areas where you need guidance.
Example: "Public speaking, industry insights, strategic planning."

Identifying Potential Board Members

Mentor: Someone with industry experience

Name: Strengths/Expertise: Why they'd be valuable on your board:

Peer: Someone at a similar career stage

Name: Strengths/Expertise: Why they'd be valuable on your board:

Industry Expert: Someone with specific knowledge or skills

Name: Strengths/Expertise: Why they'd be valuable on your board:

Diverse Perspective: Someone from a different background or field

Name: Strengths/Expertise: Why they'd be valuable on your board:

Reaching Out: Crafting Your Request

Personalized Message:
Write a draft of your message or email to potential board members.
Example: "I admire your expertise in [specific area], and I'm currently looking to build a personal board of directors to help guide my career. I would greatly appreciate the opportunity to learn from you and would value your perspective on [specific challenges]."

Meeting Setup: Schedule an initial meeting to discuss how they can support your goals.

Date/Time:

Agenda: Goals:

Roles and Responsibilities:

Cadence:

Maintaining the Relationship

Regular Check-Ins: Plan for regular check-ins with each board member.

Frequency:
(e.g., Monthly, Quarterly)

Preferred Communication Method:
(e.g., Email, Phone, In-Person)

Updates and Feedback:
Keep your board informed about your progress and challenges.
Example: "This quarter, I've focused on improving my public speaking skills and would love your feedback on my recent presentation."

Express Gratitude:
Show appreciation for their time and guidance.
Example: "Thank you for your continued support—your insights have been invaluable in helping me navigate this career transition."

Reflection and Adjustment

Assessing Impact:
Periodically assess how each board member is contributing to your growth.

Adjusting Your Board:

Consider adding new members or adjusting your board as your career evolves.

Are there areas where you need additional support?

Mentorship Kit

Mentorship Kit

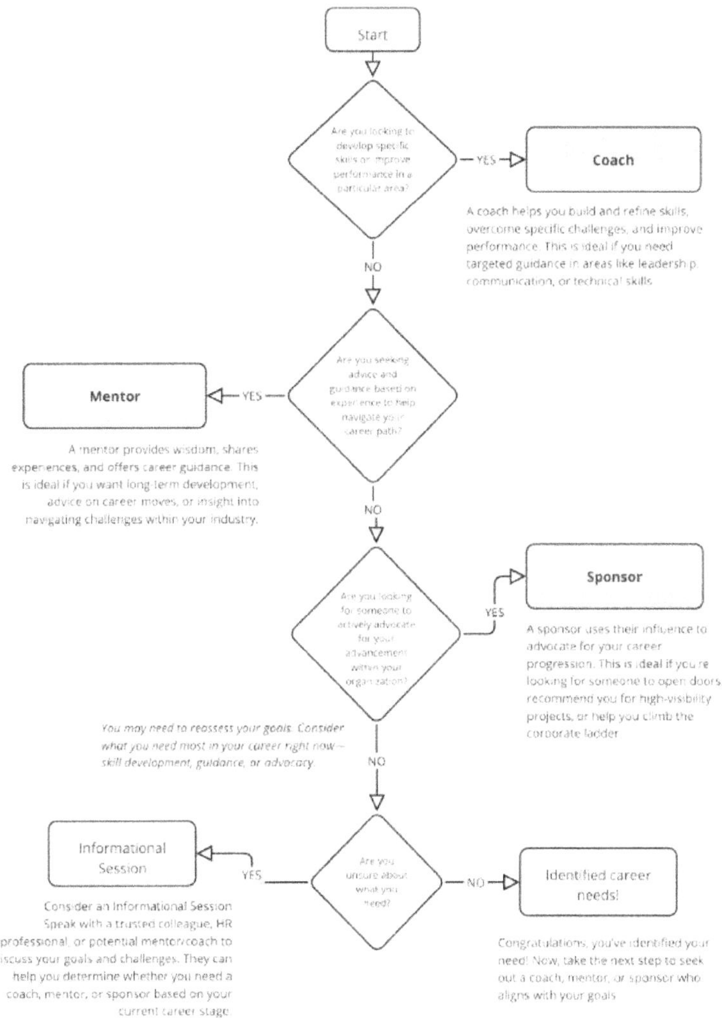

Mentorship Agreement

The Mentorship Agreement Template is designed to establish clear expectations and goals for the mentoring relationship, ensuring that both the mentor and mentee have a shared understanding of their roles, responsibilities, and objectives. This agreement serves as a foundation for building a productive and mutually beneficial partnership.

Mentor Name

Mentee Name

Duration of Mentorship

Start Date:

End Date:

Review Date:

Meeting Frequency

Preferred Meeting Schedule

Weekly •   Bi-weekly   •   Monthly•   As needed

Confidentiality Agreement

Both parties agree to maintain the confidentiality of all discussions, advice, and information shared during the mentorship. This includes personal information, professional experiences, and any sensitive matters discussed.

- The mentor and mentee will not disclose any information shared in their sessions to third parties without explicit consent from the other party.
- Any exceptions to this confidentiality (e.g., mandatory reporting of illegal activities) should be explicitly stated.

Key Objectives

**Primary Goals
for the Mentee**

1.
2.
3.

**Specific
Skills/Areas of
Focus**

1.
2.
3.

**Expected
Outcomes**

By the end of the mentorship period, the mentee
aims to have achieved the following:

1.
2.
3.

Roles and Responsibilities

**Mentor
Responsibilities:**

- Provide guidance and support on the mentee's goals.
- Share knowledge, experience, and insights relevant to the mentee's career development.
- Offer constructive feedback and encouragement.

**Mentee
Responsibilities:**

- Actively participate in meetings and discussions.
- Prepare for each session by bringing topics, questions, or challenges.
- Implement agreed-upon action items and strategies between meetings.

Communication Guidelines

Preferred Communication Methods:	Email: Phone: Other (e.g. Slack, Linkedin, etc)
Response Time Expectations:	Mentor: Respond within _ _ _ hours/days Mentee: Respond within _ _ _ hours/days
Review and Evaluation	**Midpoint Review Date:** _ *(Evaluate progress, reassess goals, and make any necessary adjustments.)*
Termination Clause	Either party may terminate the mentorship agreement with [*insert notice period, e.g., two weeks*] notice, should the relationship no longer serve the intended purpose. By signing below, both parties agree to the terms outlined in this Mentorship Agreement and commit to participating actively and respectfully in the mentorship relationship.
Signatures	Mentor Signature / Date Mentee Signature / Date

Goal-Setting

Short-term Goals

(Goals to be achieved within the next 3-6 months)

Specific Action Steps	Resource / Support Needed	Deadline	Success Measure
Goal 1:			
Goal 2:			
Goal 3:			

Long-term Goals

(Goals to be achieved within the next 1-2 years)

	Specific Action Steps	Resource / Support Needed	Deadline	Success Measure
Goal 1:				
Goal 2:				
Goal 3:				

	Specific	Measurable	Achievable	Relevant	Time-Bound
Goal 1:					
Goal 2:					
Goal 3:					

Action Plan for Each Goal

	Action Steps	Responsible Person	Support Needed	Target Completion
Goal 1:	Step 1:			
	Step 2:			
	Step 3			
Goal 2:	Step 1:			
	Step 2:			
	Step 3			
Goal 3:	Step 1:			
	Step 2:			
	Step 3			

Monitoring and Review

Review Date	Progress on Goals	Challenges Encountered	Adjustments Needed	Next Step(s)
Review 1:				
Review 2:				
Review 3:				

Meeting Agenda

The Meeting Agenda Template is designed to keep mentoring sessions focused, organized, and productive. It provides structure by outlining the topics to discuss, tracking updates on goals, and ensuring that the mentee's questions and concerns are addressed. This tool helps both the mentor and mentee make the most of their time together, facilitating meaningful and goal-oriented conversations.

Date: **Time:**

Location: **Participants:**

Purpose of the Session:

Example: "To review progress on current goals and discuss upcoming career development opportunities."

Discussion Topics

(List the topics you want to cover during this session)

Topic	Discussion Points	Time Allocation
Topic 1:		
Topic 2:		
Topic 3:		

Updates on Goals

(Review the progress of the goals set in previous sessions)

Goal	Progress Update	Challenges	Next Steps
Goal 1:			
Goal 2:			
Goal 3:			

Mentee's Questions and Concerns

(Space for the mentee to list questions or issues they want to discuss)

Question/Concern	Details	Time Allocation
Question 1:		
Question 2:		
Question 3::		

Mentor's Feedback and Advice

(Space for the mentor to provide insights, feedback, or advice based on the session's discussion)

Feedback/Advice	Related to (Goal, Question, etc.)	Actionable Steps
Advice 1:		
Advice 2:		
Advice 3:		

Action Items and Next Steps

(Summarize the key action items for both the mentor and mentee to complete before the next session)

Action Item	Responsible Person	Deadline
Item 1:		
Item 2:		
Item 3:		

Next Session Planning

Proposed Date and Time for Next Session:	
Topics for Next Session:	*Example: "Review the final version of the career development plan; discuss new challenges in current projects."*

Reflection

What went well in this session?	*Example: "We had a productive discussion on the new project and identified key areas for growth."*
What could be improved for future sessions?	*Example: "Allocate more time for discussing long-term career goals.*

Career Development Plan

A Career Development Plan is designed to help you map out your career trajectory with the input of a mentor or advisor. It will guide you through identifying the skills you need to develop, potential career paths, key milestones, and action steps to achieve your professional goals.

This provides a structured roadmap for your professional growth, with clear steps, milestones, and ongoing reflection to ensure you're staying on track to meet your career goals.

Career Vision

Define your long-term and short-term career goals.

Career Vision	Details
Long-Term Goals (5-10 years): What is your ultimate career goal? Consider job titles, industries, or leadership positions you aim to achieve.	
Short-Term Goals (1-2 years): What are your immediate professional goals? Think of promotions, skill improvements, or job changes.	

Assess Your Skills

Identify your strengths and the skills you need to develop.

Skills You Posess	Skills to Develop	*Development Opportunities*
		(e.g., courses, certifications, workshops)

Career Path Options

Explore potential career paths that align with your goals

Skills You Posess	Skills to Develop	*Development Opportunities*
		(e.g., courses, certifications, workshops)

Key Milestones

Set specific milestones to measure your progress towards your goals

Milestone	Description	Target Date	How Will You Measure Success?

Action Plan

Identify actionable steps to achieve your set career development goals

Goal	Action Steps	Resources Needed	Competion Date

Mentor Input and Feedback

Include insights or suggestions from your mentor or sponsor

Mentor's Advice	Related Goal	Steps Based on Advice

Tracking Progress

Regularly review your progress, note any adjustments needed and take time to reflect on challenges

Review Date	Progress	Challenges	Next Steps
Review 1:			
Review 2:			
Review 3:			
Review 4:			

Reflections and Adjustments

Take time to intentionally reflect on your progress and determine if any goals or strategies need adjusting.

What have you learned from pursuing these goals?

What obstacles have you encountered, and how can you address them?

Do your career goals or plans need to be revised?

Glossary of Terms

Allies and Allyship:

Allies are individuals who actively support and advocate for the rights and inclusion of marginalized groups. Allyship is the practice of using one's privilege and influence to help others by standing against discrimination and promoting equity, often by amplifying the voices and needs of those who are underrepresented or marginalized.

Bias:

Bias refers to a preconceived notion or prejudice against a person or group, often based on stereotypes rather than objective reasoning. Bias can be conscious (explicit) or unconscious (implicit), and it can affect decisions, behaviors, and interactions in ways that are unfair or discriminatory.

Burnout:

Burnout is a state of emotional, physical, and mental exhaustion caused by prolonged and excessive stress. It often occurs when someone feels overwhelmed, emotionally drained, and unable to meet constant demands, leading to a decline in performance, motivation, and well-being.

Coach:

A coach is a professional who provides guidance, support, and feedback to help individuals develop specific skills, achieve goals, and improve performance. Coaching is often focused on short-term objectives and skill development in a structured manner.

Emotional Intelligence (EQ):

Emotional intelligence is the ability to understand and manage your own emotions, as well as the emotions of others. It involves skills such as emotional awareness, empathy, and the ability to regulate emotions and respond appropriately in various situations.

Growth Mindset:

A growth mindset is the belief that abilities and intelligence can be developed through dedication, effort, and learning. Individuals with a growth mindset see challenges as opportunities to grow, embrace failures as part of the learning process, and persist in the face of setbacks.

Imposter Syndrome:

Imposter syndrome is the feeling of being a fraud or not deserving of one's achievements, despite evidence of competence and success. It often involves doubting one's abilities and fearing that others will eventually expose them as unqualified.

Mentor:

A mentor is an experienced and trusted advisor who provides guidance, support, and advice to help another person grow personally and professionally. Mentorship is typically a long-term relationship focused on broader career and personal development.

Personal Brand:

A personal brand is the unique combination of skills, experiences, and values that you present to the world. It's how you are perceived by others, both personally and professionally, and it reflects your reputation, credibility, and the value you bring to your industry or community.

Sponsor:

A sponsor is a senior leader or influential person within an organization who actively advocates for and promotes an individual's career advancement. Unlike a mentor, a sponsor uses their position and influence to create opportunities, recommend the individual for key roles, and support their professional growth.

Stereotype:

A stereotype is an oversimplified and generalized belief or idea about a particular group of people. Stereotypes are often based on assumptions rather than facts and can lead to unfair judgments and discrimination.

UVP (Unique Value Proposition):

A UVP, or Unique Value Proposition, is a clear statement that explains how your product, service, or personal brand solves a problem, fulfills a need, or delivers value in a way that sets it apart from the competition. It highlights what makes you unique and why someone should choose you over others.

Acknowledgements

To my family, especially my husband, Jon, who has been endlessly encouraging, patient, and so open-minded—learning and unlearning right alongside me. There's no one on this earth who pushes me to be a better version of myself every single day, and words cannot express the depth of my gratitude. To my kids, who challenge and inspire me daily, seeing the world through a lens of acceptance and inclusion that fills me with hope that a better world is on the horizon. And to my sister, Shabril—thank you for keeping me grounded. Even when your distractions feel ill-timed, I value them deeply because I need them, and I need you, always.

To the crap managers, bad leaders, and misogynist coworkers I've encountered along the way—thank you for showing me exactly what I don't want to be. You've helped me realize the power I carry within myself and the power we all have collectively. You won't stop us from shattering ceilings and everything else on the way to making this world a better place.

To my Latinas in Tech, my jefas—gracias de todo corazón. I spent almost two decades in tech feeling utterly alone, but this community has not only opened doors but also rekindled a deeply tucked away part of my latinidad. This incredible network of jefas and allies has unlocked so much passion and courage in me. This book is for you, inspired by you, because I want us to unlock our full potential. Esto es solo el comienzo. Vamos a cambiar el mundo, y lo vamos a hacer de una manera en que nadie se quede atrás.

To the friends who have been in my corner, cheering me on to write this book—Stacy Cassio at Pink Mentor Network and Julissa Germosén or holding me accountable, Richard R. for checking in almost every week, Albert M. for our thought-provoking discussions. Laura R., thank you for pulling me back onto a path when I strayed, got distracted, and frazzled. Kim C., Brian C., Liz G., Chelsea C., Kevin P., Ruby G., Lora M., Matt D., Patti P., Amy B., thank you for advocating, creating connections, and being my voice when I'm not in the room. And to Brett Blair, who encouraged me to finally sit down and WRITE THIS BOOK. Thank you!

And finally, to you—the reader. I want to acknowledge and thank you for picking up this book. I hope you find value in it, and if you don't, let's connect. I'd love to hear about your world, and maybe together, we can find ways to lift others up too.

Sources Consulted and Inspiration

AAUW: Empowering Women Since 1881. "Latinas and the Pay Gap." https://www.aauw.org/resources/article/latinas-and-the-pay-gap/.

Avery, Jill, and Rachel Greenwald. "A New Approach to Building Your Personal Brand." *Harvard Business Review*, May 1, 2023. https://hbr.org/2023/05/a-new-approach-to-building-your-personal-brand.

Caprino, Kathy. "Impostor Syndrome Prevalence In Professional Women And How To Overcome It." Forbes. https://www.forbes.com/sites/kathy-caprino/2020/10/22/impostor-syndrome-prevalence-in-professional-women-face-and-how-to-overcome-it/.

Dorsey, Keith D. "You're Not Powerless in the Face of Imposter Syndrome." *Harvard Business Review*, June 2, 2023. https://hbr.org/2023/06/youre-not-powerless-in-the-face-of-imposter-syndrome.

"Growth Mindset | Psychology Today." https://www.psychologytoday.com/us/basics/growth-mindset.

Langford, Joe, and Pauline Rose Clance. "The Imposter Phenomenon: Recent Research Findings Regarding Dynamics, Personality and Family Patterns and Their Implications for Treatment." *Psychotherapy: Theory, Research, Practice, Training* 30, no. 3 (1993): 495–501. https://doi.org/10.1037/0033-3204.30.3.495.

"NSF's NCSES Releases Report on Diversity Trends in STEM Workforce and Education | NSF - National Science Foundation," January 30, 2023. https://new.nsf.gov/news/diversity-and-stem-2023.

"What Is a Growth Mindset? | Coursera." https://www.coursera.org/articles/growth-mindset.

Stacy Whitenight is an innovative Business Operations Executive celebrated for her dynamic approach to enhancing operational efficiency and spearheading transformative projects. With a robust background in Agile methodologies and cloud technologies, she excels in navigating the complexities of modern business landscapes, ensuring the seamless delivery of impactful features at scale. Stacy's career is marked by significant achievements, including generating substantial revenue growth, optimizing operational processes, and salvaging key customer relationships through strategic interventions.

Holding certifications in Project Management (PMP) and Change Management from Cornell University, along with a Masters in Technology and Instruction from George Mason University, Stacy is a lifelong learner. Her academic pursuits have equipped her with a unique blend of technical know-how and strategic acumen, enabling her to align technological solutions with creative approaches to solve intricate business challenges. This skill set was instrumental in leading a cross-functional team to successfully launch a global cloud migrations initiative, integrating tens of thousands of users into a new digital ecosystem.

A multi-cultural and bilingual tech enthusiast, Stacy infuses her diverse heritage into her work, driving expansive innovation and fostering an inclusive environment that values every individual's contribution. With aspirations of becoming a COO, she is inspired by the operational excellence of companies like the Walt Disney Company and is dedicated to creating customer-centric experiences that resonate on a global scale.

Beyond her professional expertise, Stacy's leadership style is characterized by coaching and mentoring, emphasizing the importance of team empowerment and data-driven decision-making. Her executive presence is bolstered by her proficiency in a wide array of tools and software, from Agile and Scrum frameworks to advanced data analysis and web development platforms. Stacy is passionate about Diversity, Equity, and Inclusion, advocating for strategies that enhance organizational belonging and equity.

Outside the office, Stacy's life is as vibrant and diverse as her career. A former D1 NCAA Athlete, she enjoys exploring the world, hitting the golf course, snowboarding, and engaging in sports like soccer or flag football. An avid 3D printing enthusiast, Stacy delights in cosplaying, often accompanied by her family and two golden retrievers. Her personal interests mirror her professional journey—constantly pushing boundaries, embracing new challenges, and finding joy in innovation and exploration.